ABORIGINAL ENVIRONMENTAL IMPACTS

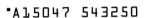

ABORIGINAL ENVIRONMENTAL IMPACTS

James L. Kohen

UNSW
PRESS

Published by
University of New South Wales Press
Sydney 2052 Australia

Telephone (02) 398 8900
Fax (02) 398 3408

National Library of Australia
Cataloguing-in-Publication entry:

Kohen, J. L.
    Aboriginal environmental impacts.

    Bibliography.
    Includes index.
    ISBN 0 86840 301 6.

    1. Aborigines, Australian – Social life and customs.
    2. Land use – Environmental aspects – Australia. I. Title.

304.20899915

Available in North America through:
ISBS
Portland, OR 97213–3644, USA
Tel: (503) 287 3093 Fax: (503) 280 8832

Available in Singapore, Malaysia & Brunei through:
Publishers Marketing Services
Singapore 1232
Tel: (65) 256 5166 Fax: (65) 253 0008

Printed by Southwood Press Pty Limited
80 – 92 Chapel Street, Marrickville, NSW 2204

Contents

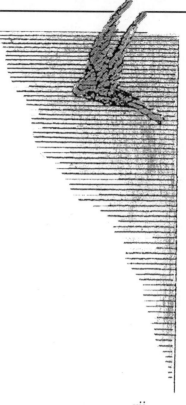

Introduction

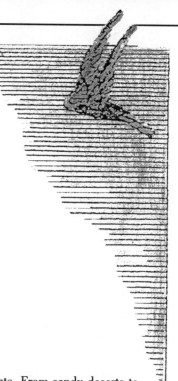

Australia is a land of varied environments. From sandy deserts to rainforests, and from snow-covered alps to scorching salt lakes, it offers a unique range of habitats. Non-Aboriginal Australians have had a great deal of difficulty in finding ways to successfully exploit many of these places. When the more extreme environments are used, it is generally for brief visits and certainly not for permanent occupation. More than 80% of the Australian population live along a thin coastal strip in the southeast stretching from Brisbane to Adelaide.

Before European settlement, the southeast also supported the highest population density of Aboriginal people, but in stark contrast to non-Aboriginal settlement, Aboriginal Australians had adapted to virtually every environment across the continent. In the late eighteenth century, when Europeans first began to spread out from Port Jackson, Aborigines were hunting and gathering in almost every major ecosystem, and even those inhospitable places which were no longer used, like parts of southwest Tasmania and Kangaroo Island, had supported Aboriginal populations in the past.[1]

Archaeological evidence now suggests that Aboriginal people have occupied Australia for over 50,000 years, and possibly much longer. During this time, they have come to understand the land, to the extent that their spiritual beliefs about the land extend beyond any European sense of ownership. Aboriginal people see themselves as a part of the land, and as a consequence they have duties and obligations directed towards the conservation and protection of their particular 'country'.

Yet there exists a range of opinion on how much this interaction between Aboriginal people and the landscape impacted physically and biologically on that landscape. David Horton argues that Aboriginal people have had little or no environmental impact.[2] At the other end of the spectrum of opinion, one of the most extreme views is that of Rhys Jones, who first coined the term 'firestick farming' for the way which he believed fire was used by Aboriginal people as a tool for modifying their environment. Essentially, Jones believes that Aborigines dramatically modified the distribution and abundance of Australia's flora and fauna by their intensive and systematic use of fire.[3]

The relationship between Aborigines and the environment was observed by Sir Thomas Mitchell in 1839, when he recorded:

> Fire, grass and kangaroos, and human inhabitants, seem all dependent on each other for existence in Australia; for any one of these being wanting, the others could no longer continue. Fire is necessary to burn the grass, and form those open forests, in which we find the large forest-kangaroo; the native applies the fire to the grass at certain seasons, in order that a young green crop may subsequently spring up, and so attract and enable him to kill or take the kangaroo with nets.[4]

Tim Flannery from the Australian Museum has argued that Aborigines hunted most of Australia's large animals to extinction, and that Aboriginal burning practices were used subsequently to increase the productivity of the landscape following the removal of virtually all of the large herbivores.[5]

All of these arguments fail to recognise that Aboriginal technology was not static over the 50,000 years of occupation. The technology changed, particularly during the last 5000 years. There is strong evidence for major Aboriginal population increase during this period. The dingo arrived around 4000 years ago, almost certainly as a domesticated animal, and it clearly had a dramatic impact on the population of many other mammals, eating some and competing with others, including Aboriginal people. Archaeological sites show that stone-tipped and barbed spears for hunting became important and dominated prehistoric sites across the country, and then became less important, with some types of specialised stone tools disappearing altogether. New fishing technologies spread across the continent. Edge-ground axes, which were common in the north more than 20,000 years ago, suddenly spread south and became an important item of material culture and trade in the south-east. Many new camp sites were occupied for the first time, and earlier sites were occupied much more intensively. Interestingly, few researchers seem to have related these technological changes to Aboriginal use of fire, implying that burning practices were an aspect of Aboriginal technology which arrived 50,000 years ago and which has continued to be used in much the same manner ever since. The evidence suggests otherwise.

By the time Europeans began to recognise the complexity of the relationship between Aboriginal people and their land, there had already been large-scale depopulations. Yet the evidence, both ethnographic and archaeological, is clear. Aboriginal people were practising incipient agriculture and animal husbandry. They were living in complex socioeconomic systems which required co-operation to maximise the productivity of the landscape. Their method of supporting their population was based on the concept of 'sustainable development', the ability to regenerate resources so they would be available for future generations. Their spiritual and religious beliefs reinforced this view of the world.

But just as Aboriginal technology was not static, neither was the environment in which they existed. Animal populations changed in response to new hunting techniques and the addition of a new predator, the dingo. The boundaries of vegetation associations were modified by the use of mosaic burning to increase the productivity of the landscape. The fire-induced habitats supported different faunal associations, and over time these almost certainly varied in response to hunting pressure. Clearly there was a dynamic relationship between Aboriginal people, their technology, the flora and the fauna. One consequence of this dynamic was that Aboriginal people clearly impacted on the Australian environment in a number of ways, but without causing any of the large-scale land degradation which typifies more recent European land-management practices. Perhaps non-Aboriginal Australians have something to learn from 50,000 years of Aboriginal land management practices.

CHAPTER 1

Australia before Man

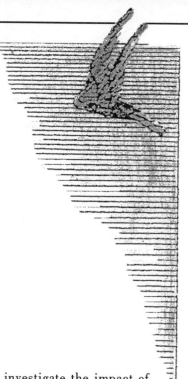

The principal aim of this book is to investigate the impact of Aboriginal Australians on the Australian environment. In order to understand human impacts, it is first necessary to understand the nature and variety of habitats within Australia, and in particular to identify any special adaptations of Australian flora and fauna which may have occurred because of the relative isolation of the Australian continent from the rest of the world. This involves at least a limited understanding of Australian biogeography and the subsequent evolution of plants and animals within Australia.

Biogeography is the study of the distribution of living organisms. Some species of plants and animals have narrow distributions, while others are widespread. Biogeography tries to answer not only the question 'what lives where?', but also 'why does it live there?' and 'how did it get there?' Biogeography therefore incorporates not only the study of present and past distributions of plants and animals, but also the study of the movement of land masses which produced the distribution of the continents as we see them today.

The biota of any particular location consists of the particular species which inhabit particular environmental niches. In any forest, certain plants and animals will occupy similar niches, and the species which fill the niche will be determined by the biogeographical history of the area. Other factors which will influence the distribution of plants and animals include geology, topography and climate.

Biogeographic Regions

There are six broad zoogeographical regions of the world. These are the Nearctic Region (North America); the Neotropic Region (South America); the Ethiopian Region (most of Africa); the Palaearctic Region (consisting of northern Africa, Europe, and northern Asia); the Oriental Region (which includes India, China and South-East Asia); and the Australian Region. These regions are generally separated by some kind of physical barrier — a major ocean, a high mountain range, or perhaps a desert.

Depending on the particular plant or animal, what is a barrier to one species may not be a barrier to another. For a lowland animal, a mountain range is a major barrier to movement; to a warm-water animal, a cold current can prevent migration. For most land mammals, the most important barriers are wide bodies of water.

It is worth recognising the fact that what is now a barrier may not have been so in the past. In the past 20,000 years, the Nearctic and the Palaearctic regions have been linked across the Bering land bridge between Alaska and Siberia, and this allowed movement of land-based mammals from one side to the other. Man was one of the terrestrial mammals which moved from west to east across this bridge to colonise the Americas. In Australia, until around 12,000 years ago, Papua-New Guinea, Tasmania and Kangaroo Island were all part of one land mass, Sahul. They were cut off from the mainland as the sea levels rose at the end of the last ice age.

Understanding Australian biogeography involves the study of evolution, selection, competition and extinction, superimposed over long-term geological processes like continental drift and climatic fluctuations.

Continental Drift

Wegener's theory of continental drift explains the present distribution of the world's land masses. Until about 200 million years ago, all of the major continents were held together, locked up in a supercontinent known as Pangaea. This broke into two groups: one in the north, called Laurasia; and one in the south called Gondwana. This southern supercontinent, Gondwana, consisting of Africa–South America, Australia–Antarctica and India, existed until around 190 million years ago, when the various components broke up and began to drift in different directions. India drifted northwards, and ran into Asia about 50 million years ago. Around the same time, New Zealand separated from Australia. The fossil evidence confirms that Australia, Antarctica and South America were all components of this land mass. In only two parts of the world did the marsupials radiate to any great extent — Australia and South America. Indeed, the evidence is strong that at least some common marsupial species gave rise to both Australian and South American radiations.

The post-Gondwana history of Australia is one of relative stability. As it drifted northward into the Pacific, few mountain ranges were built, and those which were created were relatively low. There was not a great deal of tectonic activity and it was located at the centre of a continental plate. As a result, Australia became a relatively flat continent. This had great implications as the sea levels rose and fell during the Pleistocene, because large areas of land were first flooded and then exposed. Where the rainfall was relatively constant, the surface weathered and the soils became acidic. Laterisation bound up nutrients like phosphorus, impoverishing the soil and removing several trace elements which were essential for the growth of many plant species. New landscapes arose only as the result of erosion of old ones. Without tectonic change or glaciation, the Australian landscape was changed only by erosion.[1]

Plant Biogeography

One of the consequences of poor soil fertility was that the vegetation which existed on the Australian continent diversified and filled the niches created by poor-quality soils. There are more plant species growing on the Hawkesbury sandstone around Sydney than grow in many European countries.

The old Gondwana forests had been dominated by gymnosperms — the conifers, *Auracaria* and podocarps, but just as Gondwana broke up, the flowering plants, the angiosperms, began to radiate. Because of the large size and climatic diversity which existed within Gondwana, the vegetation associations were varied, and when Australia separated it took with it enough angiosperms to expand and almost fill the entire continent.

There are still a few remnant auracarian forests in Australia, but over most of the continent it is the angiosperms which have dominated. *Nothofagus*, the Antarctic beech, was one of the early angiosperms which was present on Gondwana when Australia became isolated. Minor families included the Myrtaceae, the grasses, the Xanthorhhoeas, and chenopods. A few of the genera which were present and which to become important included the *Banksia*, *Eucalyptus*, *Hakea* and *Melaleuca*. Similar vegetation associations characterised parts of Antarctica, South America and New Zealand. Where the rainfall was year round and moderately high, rainforests were maintained, but the minor flora adapted and speciated, filling many of the niches in the drier areas.

Although there were a few late plant invasions from southeast Asia in the tropical north, most of these are restricted to Papua-New Guinea, and Australia's broad plant associations have remained essentially isolated for about 30 million years. During that time, the plants have radiated, speciated and adapted to one of the most diverse climatic regimes in the world. The mountains of Papua-New Guinea and the ocean barriers acted as filters to the plant species in the same way that they prevented the spread of animals.

The slow movement to the north and the climatic fluctuations broke up the rainforests into smaller patches, each of which then speciated in its own way. Australia became a dry continent. Australian aridity was 'seasonal, episodic and chronic'.[2] It became, in places, part of the annual wet and dry season. In other places there would be drought extending over several years. The moisture-loving vegetation became crowded along the coastal fringe, with the Great Dividing Range acting as an effective barrier to water movement. To the east of the ranges it was wet; to the west of the ranges it was dry, and became drier further to the west.

This process continued during the Pleistocene, the last 2 million years, and the result was that some of the previously minor components of the Australian vegetation became dominant over much of the country. Those plants which could adapt to dry conditions, the scleromorphs, flourished. These were the plants with small tough leathery leaves, which reduced water loss and allowed the plant to conserve nutrients as well as water. The other aspect of these leaves was that, being relatively dry, and often filled with oil, they had the capacity to burn much more readily and violently than the leaves of the moist forest species.

In Australian forests, the evergreens dominate — it is unwise to be a deciduous tree if you're growing in a nutrient-deficient soil or in an arid environment. The *Nothofagus* and *Podocarpus* rainforests contracted to the moist cool southeast. *Casuarina* replaced *Auracaria*. Grasses replaced ferns in the understorey, forests were replaced by woodlands, which became dominated by eucalypts and wattles. It was climatic change which resulted in a massive radiation in the scleromorphs, creating the Australian vegetation much as we know it today.

By 38,000 years ago the Auracarian rainforests had just about all disappeared, and *Casuarina* was beginning to be replaced by eucalypts. Around this time, there is a massive increase in the amount of charcoal found in pollen cores obtained from deep lakes in north Queensland — probably because the new sclerophyll vegetation under dry conditions provided an abundant source of fuel.[3] Whether the cause of the fires which produced the charcoal was natural or man-made is subject to debate, but by around 38,000 years ago Aboriginal people were well-established in Australia. By the time Aborigines first arrived, the Australian vegetation was already highly specialised to cope with arid conditions, and also highly likely to catch fire. Some components of the Australian vegetation have been described as 'fire-requirers' or, more importantly, 'fire-promoters'.[4]

During the late Pleistocene, as the great ice sheets expanded and contracted in the Northern Hemisphere, the distribution of plants also varied across Australia. Lakes formed, expanded, contracted and finally dried out in many parts of southeastern Australia. Woodlands became grasslands as temperatures fell, rainfall halved and fire became less significant. Around 18,000 years ago, the ice reached its greatest extent, the sea levels were low and Australia was joined to Papua-New Guinea and Tasmania.

With the climatic warming which took place during the late Pleistocene and the Holocene, the ice sheets melted, sea levels rose, rainfall increased along the coasts and in the tropical north during the summer monsoons, and dense rainforests became re-established along the Queensland coast.

The warm conditions of the Holocene, over the last 10,000 years, provided a period of climatic stability which was unusual in the recent history of the Australian landscape.

Animal Biogeography

Once the supercontinents had separated, adaptive radiation in one region occurred independently of any radiation which was occurring in the other biogeographical regions. In each region, parallel evolution was likely to take place, because each of the major ecological niches would need to be filled by an animal with similar requirements and characteristics.

The Australian region was unique in that it had separated from the adjoining biogeographical regions before the first major radiation of the placental mammals. Consequently, although there do appear to have been a few primitive eutherians present in Australia, based on fossils found in the last few years, there was no massive radiation of this group.[5] Indeed, the indigenous eutherian mammals of Australia became extinct and the only eutherians other than the bats, which could fly, are relatively recent arrivals. Instead, the radiation occurred within two other groups of mammals, the monotremes and the marsupials.

Two characteristics of insular faunas, impoverishment and endemicity, are obvious when the make-up of the Australian fauna is examined. The number of terrestrial mammal orders present in Australia, at least until Europeans arrived, is five (not including humans). Even the island of Madagascar has six mammal orders. Asia and Africa each have twelve orders. The five Australian orders include the bats and rodents, while the only eutherian carnivore found in Australia is a recent immigrant, the dingo. There are only two extant species of monotremes, the echidna and the platypus. Therefore the great majority of ecological niches for land animals are filled by marsupials, and all of them are endemic to Australia (east of Wallace's Line).

There is no evidence to suggest that the dingo existed in Australia prior to around 4000 years ago. If the dingo was introduced into Australia as a domesticated animal which arrived along with humans, this is a unique case of a population that had passed through a stage of domestication and some degree of artificial selection and had then fully returned to the status of a wild species through many generations in isolation. This kind of a history may have had unusual genetic and adaptive consequences.[6] Regardless of this, it is clear that once the dingo arrived in Australia it had a fairly dramatic impact on the indigenous fauna. Certainly it competed with the thylacine and the Tasmanian Devil, both of which then existed on the mainland, but it may also have competed with another carnivore in Australia, the Aboriginal people.

All the native rodents in the Australian Region belong to one family, the Muridae, which includes water rats, rats and mice. However, all of these animals were probably derived from a single ancestral immigrant. It seems that the rodents reached Papua-New Guinea and Australia by island-hopping from southeast Asia, and then diverged, possibly taking over from some small marsupials which occupied similar niches.

Australia has a good range of bats, but this is not really surprising, as bats can fly over ocean barriers. Because of this, many of the Australian bats are not endemic, so, in terms of understanding Australian biogeography, they are of limited value.

Monotremes

The two monotremes which survived in Australia until the arrival of Europeans, the platypus and the echidna, are the only survivors of the primitive group of mammals which lay eggs. Each fits into an ecological niche which has its analogue in other continents. Each animal is the only surviving species in Australia, although there are other species of echidna in Papua-New Guinea.

Marsupials

It is within the marsupials that we see the greatest radiation within the Australian fauna. Small, medium and large herbivores are represented by the hare wallabies, potoroos, wallabies and kangaroos; arboreal animals are represented by the possums, gliders, phascogales and the koala; terrestrial animals include the numbat (an insectivore), and the wombat (a herbivore); carnivorous animals include the thylacine (Tasmanian tiger), Tasmanian devil and the native cats.[7] Indeed, just about every ecological niche which is occupied by a eutherian mammal outside Australia is occupied by a marsupial inside Australia.

Thirty or forty thousand years ago, there existed an even greater array of diverse forms, including the equivalents of the giant herbivores like the elephants and hippopotamus, in the form of the Diprotodontids, and leopard-like tree dwelling carnivores in the form of *Thylacoleo*, the marsupial lion.

There are some striking examples of convergent evolution in Australia. Eutherian dog-like carnivores are found in every other biogeographical region, but in Australia a marsupial, the thylacine, evolved to fill the niche. Superficially, the thylacine is very dog-like or wolf-like, but biologically elephants and mice are more closely related. In South America, a marsupial borhyaenid evolved to fill the same niche, but it became extinct when eutherian carnivores crossed the Panama Isthmus from the north, following volcanic activity which linked the two American continents.[8] In the same way, the thylacine became extinct on the mainland when the dingo arrived, although the reasons for this extinction are not altogether clear.

With a range of animals filling each of these niches 50,000 years ago, the transition of a human population from the Oriental zone to the Australian zone would not necessarily create any major economic pressure for the humans because, although the animals were different, and were marsupials rather than placental animals, they were occupying essentially equivalent niches to those placentals which were found in southeast Asia.

When Aboriginal people first arrived in Australia, even the vegetation in the far north was very similar to what they had encountered in island southeast Asia. Rainforest was to be found on both sides of the ocean barrier which separated Australia and Papua-New Guinea from southeast Asia. It was only when they travelled south into the arid zone that major floristic and faunal changes would have been evident.

It seems likely that the change from southeast Asia to Australia would not have been as dramatic as might first be imagined.[9] Indeed, if, as has been suggested, the ancestors of Australian Aboriginal populations were island-dwellers, then coastal food resources would have been, to all intents and purposes, identical. There is no reason to assume that the original colonisers would have had any great difficulty rapidly adapting to the Australian continent, at least until they moved into the semi-arid and arid zone. Even then, the climate 50,000 years ago was probably not as extreme as the one we see there today.

CHAPTER 2

The first arrivals

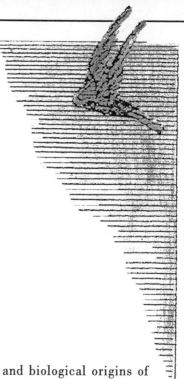

In any discussion of the geographic and biological origins of Aboriginal people, it is wise to state the cultural bias which influences the discussion. I have been raised in a Eurocentric, Christian society, and educated in the discipline of science. This has bestowed upon me many inherent biases and prejudices. I have a personal belief system which may or may not coincide with others in my society, and that is my right within an egalitarian society.

In the same way, Aboriginal people have a right to maintain their culturally and socially determined beliefs, one of which deals with their origins and creation. Indeed, it may be said that the belief in the Dreaming extends far beyond an explanation of their origins, because it explains the origins and existence of everything in the world, everything in the past and everything in the future. The following discussion is my perception of the origins of Aboriginal people, but at the same time I recognise the fact that traditional Aboriginal beliefs maintain that Aboriginal people have always been in Australia, since it was first created in the Dreaming. The two belief systems, one based on scientific principles and one based on traditional Aboriginal religious beliefs, can happily coexist, and there is no conflict between them.

Origins of Aboriginal people

In order to understand how Aboriginal people may have impacted on the Australian environment, it is necessary to understand how Aboriginal prehistory relates to the broader study of human prehistory, including the evolution of our own species. It is necessary to move well away from the Australian region to understand the processes of human evolution. While it is generally accepted that we, as a species, began our evolutionary experience on the African continent, that is about all that is agreed. Certainly by about 5 million years ago, the human line had diverged from the common line which led to our closest living relative, the chimpanzee, and by 4 million years ago one of our ancestors, *Australopithecus afarensis*, had become bipedal. This species subsequently diverged into a number of different species of Australopithecines, some omnivorous and some herbivorous.[1]

Homo habilis

By 2 million years ago, a tool-making descendant of *Australopithecus afarensis* was scavenging around central Africa. It had a brain capacity larger than the Australopithecines at around 670 cc, and a rounded skull with reduced brow ridges. This hominid was *Homo habilis*, the earliest representative of our genus. *Homo habilis* was a part-time carnivore, and certainly coexisted with the robust Australopithecines for at least half a million years, but probably did not compete directly for food. The Australopithecines' vegetarian diet was not shared by *Homo habilis*, who moved towards active hunting of prey as well as scavenging. At this stage of human evolution, the use of stone tools became of great importance in the evolutionary process. Simple stone artefacts have been found in many early African sites, at least some of which appear to have been used for processing meat and smashing bones.

Like *Australopithecus africanus*, another descendant of *Australopithecus afarensis*, *Homo habilis* was relatively short-lived, and by about 1.5 million years ago had been replaced by a new species, *Homo erectus*. The Australopithecine line became extinct about 1 million years ago, but *Homo erectus* proved to be a far more durable and adaptable species.

Homo erectus

Homo erectus was the first hominid to move out of Africa. The remains of *Homo erectus* have been found from Europe across Asia to China and Indonesia, where the two most famous groups of hominid fossils have been found; Peking man and Java man. This species can also claim several other firsts, including the use of a wider range of stone tools including handaxes, the use of fire for cooking and keeping warm, the intense use of caves, and organised active hunting activities.

The earliest *Homo erectus* remains are dated at about 1.5 million years ago, and over the next million years the brain size increased from around 800 cc to about 1100 cc. This was the only major physical change which occurred, for *Homo erectus* already had most of the characteristics we think of as being human. The pelvis and lower limbs were fully adapted for bipedal locomotion, and *Homo erectus* was well developed to survive in his environment of tropical and temperate forests.

There are two main facial features which make it easy to recognise the skull of *Homo erectus*. These are the heavy brow ridges and receding forehead, and the large size of the teeth and palate, suggesting that the diet was still varied and included a substantial amount of tough vegetable material. *Homo erectus* may have hunted, but he was certainly not an exclusive carnivore.

The movement of *Homo erectus* into the colder parts of the world marks an important step in human evolution. For the first time, an animal could survive in an environment which was hostile, not by biological adaptation through evolution, but by technological and social adaptation. An animal which had evolved in tropical climates and which had lost its hair as an adaptation to life on the savannah could now survive in a range of new environments by putting on the hair of some other animal. It is also probably at this point that knowledge acquired by one generation was passed on to the next. The evolution of human culture had begun. Stone tools took on a wider range, and specialised stone tools were produced (although the tradition of handaxe manufacture continued for over a million years and is found in many parts of the world where *H. erectus* is found). *Homo erectus* built huts and wore animal skins, and clearly was the first to use intellectual capacities to short-circuit the evolutionary process.

By a million years ago, a new technology had been acquired — fire. Fire was probably obtained accidentally from a natural source of ignition, perhaps lightning. Most animals have a fear of fire, and humans are the only animal to use it directly. It is a multipurpose tool — it is used to keep warm, to cook food, and to keep predators at bay. *Homo erectus* lived both in the open in shelters (which required additional technological skills to manufacture), and in caves and rock overhangs. Their social network enabled cooperative hunting and a degree of specialisation in the division of labour. If it is possible to extend the ethnographic analogy back half a million years, then even at this early stage males were probably the hunters of larger game and females the collectors of small game and gatherers of fruit and roots.

A characteristic of all human species is that they are cooperative social animals. A strict division of labour is unusual in the animal world, but there is a firm biological basis for some distinction between the roles of male and female animals. In humans, males are larger, stronger and faster, whereas females are smaller and better able to store fatty tissue. These factors are probably determined by the need for women to be able to become pregnant and bear young, and the long human gestation period means that a lot of time and energy is invested by females in this process. Even from this early stage, males and females are likely to have had different kinds of impacts on the local environment.

With the spread of *Homo erectus*, the increase in population, the use of fire and the exploitation of a greater variety of plant and animal resources, the impact of humans on the environment had certainly become more significant, but it was still limited and geographically localised. Population densities were low and it is unlikely that fire was used in any directed way to modify the landscape, but there is some evidence to suggest that even at these early phases of human evolution, *Homo erectus* may have caused some local extinctions of animals.

The fauna of Java 500,000 years ago included elephants, giant water buffalo, large monitor lizards and a huge land tortoise, with a shell two metres long. Shortly after human cultural remains occur in the palaeontological record, the tortoise disappears. It has been speculated that such an easy prey would have rapidly succumbed to a new predator which had the capacity to turn the animal upside down to kill it.[2]

One other interesting point about the Javan *Homo erectus* is that there is no evidence for a stone tool industry associated with their fossil remains. Thorne has speculated that this may be because sharp cutting tools were not made with stone, but of bamboo, which can produce razor-sharp edges.[3] Organic materials are poorly preserved in the archaeological record, so if bamboo was being used it would be very difficult to detect. This is an example of man adapting to the immediate environment and using natural resources which are locally available as a substitute for other more traditional resources which are not.

Homo sapiens

Homo sapiens came into existence between 500,000 and 200,000 years ago. There are many palaeoanthropologists who will argue that there should be no distinction made between *Homo erectus* and *Homo sapiens*, and that they are one in the same species. Regardless of the biological basis for this suggestion, there do appear to be many cultural differences. With the evolution of our species came a greater degree of sophistication in the stone tools, and a greater flexibility in strategies for surviving in a wider range of environments.

The actual point of transition between *Homo erectus* and *Homo sapiens* is not easy to determine, but by 200,000 years ago there were forms not significantly different from modern humans, perhaps close enough to be placed in our own species. The intermediate forms such as the fossils from Swanscombe in England and Steinheim in Germany gave rise to a culturally distinct group, the Neanderthals, named after the Neander Valley in Germany where fossils and stone tools were found in the 1850s. Neanderthal man is now considered to be a subspecies of *Homo sapiens*, with the full taxonomic title *Homo sapiens neanderthalensis*.

The stone toolkit of Neanderthal man was more advanced, with a wider range of specialised flake tools, some of which were used for preparing animal skins for clothes, necessary because the Neanderthals lived during a period of geological time dominated by the ice ages. The Neanderthals did not retreat with the advancing ice, but remained in northern Europe and Asia to successfully adapt to the new environmental regime. Neanderthal fossils and cultural remains have been found throughout Africa, Asia and Europe, but in Europe they were suddenly replaced around 35,000 years ago by a new subspecies, *Homo sapiens sapiens*, modern man. In many caves and rock shelters, the transition between the two groups is almost instantaneous.

The period between 100,000 and 40,000 years ago is one of the most interesting phases of human prehistory. Not only were the Neanderthals replaced in Europe, but the first major ocean voyages were taking place. The ancestors of Aboriginal Australians had arrived in Sahul, a land mass which included Australia and Papua-New Guinea. This was the first occasion that hominids had managed to cross a substantial ocean barrier.

The new subspecies was also able to adapt to the cold conditions in northern Europe. There is still some debate as to whether the Neanderthals were forced out of Europe by more culturally sophisticated people coming from the east, or whether there was a mingling of the genes and the Neanderthals interbred with the newcomers. However, the most recent genetic evidence suggests that all *Homo sapiens sapiens* are probably derived from a small number of individuals who had originated in Africa by around 200,000 years ago, and who subsequently spread throughout the world replacing other existing human populations.[4]

Recently, sites in Africa and the Middle East have been described which contain modern man, *Homo sapiens sapiens*, dating to 90,000 years ago. If these early dates are confirmed, the replacement of the Neanderthals by modern man is not the simple process it was once thought to be, for the two subspecies coexisted for perhaps 60,000 years.[5] This has important implications when we come to discuss the Australian fossil evidence.

Homo sapiens, like his predecessor *Homo erectus*, was a hunter and a gatherer. His social organisation gave him a distinct advantage over other carnivores. His intelligence allowed him to successfully plan and execute hunts, and to forecast when and where herds of game would be found. His intellectual capacity could also be directed towards things other than the concern for survival. The last 30,000 years have seen an enormous growth in human cultural diversity.

One of the problems we face in understanding the process of human evolution, particularly in southeast Asia and Australia, is that there is so little fossil evidence. There is clearly some evidence of *Homo sapiens* in Java dated to between 150,000 and 200,000 years ago from Ngandong on the Solo River, but there is little direct fossil evidence from the past 200,000 years. Few significant human fossils have been found in southeast Asia which date between 150,000 and 10,000 years ago, a time period which is critical in terms of the origins of Aboriginal people.[6]

In much the same way, there is little hard evidence from China. There are also a few fossils dated from between 150,000 and 200,000 years ago which appear to be early *Homo sapiens*, and fossils dating to 60,000 years ago are clearly *Homo sapiens*, but there is a lack of information on the intervening period.[7]

There are two basic approaches to recent human evolution — the 'Out of Africa' hypothesis, and the 'multiregional' approach. If we accept the view of Wolpoff and Thorne, there is evidence within the Chinese *Homo erectus* fossils for a gradual change towards *Homo sapiens* over time. Their view is that *Homo erectus* at Zhoukoudian show an evolution over perhaps 250,000 years towards a more human appearance. Thorne suggests that modern Asians evolved in Asia, and argues that it was these people, the descendants of the Chinese *Homo erectus*, which evolved into *Homo sapiens* and spread throughout southeast Asia. Similarly, he argues, with even less direct evidence, that the *Homo erectus* populations of southeast Asia also evolved into more 'modern' forms, eventually becoming *Homo sapiens*.[8]

Wolpoff and Thorne are the main supporters of the multiregional hypothesis. Their view is not shared by many researchers, most of whom believe that both fossil and biochemical evidence support the

evolution of modern *Homo sapiens sapiens* from an isolated population in Africa, which subsequently spread throughout the rest of the
world, replacing all other existing human populations. The isolation
of the modern human population is believed to have occurred around
200,000 years ago, but recent research suggests that the widespread
replacement of populations may have begun as recently as 60,000 to
100,000 years ago. Regardless of which view is correct, if the ancestors of Aboriginal people first colonised Australia around 50–60,000
years ago, or even 100,000 years ago, then they were clearly *Homo
sapiens*. There would be no real argument about the origins of
Aboriginal people had it not been for the discovery of a number of
rather unusual human fossil skulls in various parts of Australia.

Aboriginal colonisation

It is clear that, in order to reach Sahul, the enlarged continental mass
continent which consisted of Australia, New Guinea and Tasmania,
even at the period of lowest sea level 53,000 years ago, several long sea
crossings would have been necessary, including one of at least 80 km.
This suggests that the initial colonisation was probably accidental, and
may well have occurred as a single event. It was almost certainly pre-
ceded by a period of island-hopping across the islands of Indonesia,
although it is worth remembering that the low sea levels also joined
much of southeast Asia into a large land mass, referred to as Sunda.

There is an often-quoted example of how many people may have
landed on the first arrival. One theory suggests that 'one pregnant
woman floating on a log' is enough to populate the entire continent.
However, a number of computer simulations have been carried out
which suggest that at least six to ten people (three to five couples)
would be required to have a statistically sound probability of establish-
ing a population, assuming monogamy. If the requirement for
monogamy was relaxed, the simulation suggested that five couples
would have a 75% chance of successfully colonising a new continent.
This indicates that a single canoe or raft blown off course on a short trip
could provide enough people to populate the Australian continent.[9]

Probably the most important question to be answered is: exactly
when did Aborigines arrive? By looking at the fluctuations in sea
level, it is possible to determine when the periods of low sea level
occurred, and therefore what periods were most likely for Aboriginal
people to first reach Australia.

Although there were some phases of low sea level more than
100,000 years ago, there is no archaeological evidence to suggest that
Aboriginal people had arrived at this early period. The earliest dated

human occupation sites in Australia are at Malakunanja II and Malangangerr, both on the Arnhem Land escarpment.[10] There is no charcoal available for dating the lowest levels of these shelters, but thermoluminescence dates suggest that both sites were first occupied between 45,000 and 61,000 years ago, with the mean estimate around 53,000 years ago. This coincides with a period of low sea level. There have been some criticisms of the interpretation of the data for these two sites, but the claim is a strong one and fits within the broad range of dates which seem likely on the basis of other dated sites.

The oldest site dated by radiocarbon is at Upper Swan near Perth. Here a consistent series of radiocarbon dates from hearths suggest that Aboriginal occupation of the area had begun by around 40,000 years ago. The dates range between 38,000 and 42,000.[11] However, these dates are right at the limit of resolution of radiocarbon dating, and a tiny amount of contamination by modern carbon can give a date which is too recent. If Aborigines were near Perth 40,000 years ago, then they must have arrived somewhat earlier further to the north.

There is another southern site which may well date to more than 40,000 years ago. At Keilor in Victoria, stone artefacts have been found in terraces which appear to date to between 36,000 and 45,000 years ago, although the evidence for a very early date is rather weak.[12]

However, in western New South Wales, particularly at Lake Mungo, there is abundant evidence for Aboriginal exploitation of aquatic resources between 35,000 and 40,000 years ago, and there are dates for Tasmania which suggest that Aboriginal people had walked the length of the continent by 30,000 years ago.

The period of low sea level at 53,000 years ago would seem to be the most likely time for the arrival of Aboriginal people in Australia. There have been claims of older sites. In Victoria, it has been suggested that a shell midden was made by humans around 70,000 years ago, while there are presumed stone artefacts coming from river terraces again around 70,000 years old.[13] There is also a period of relatively low sea level around this time.

In summary, Aboriginal people probably originated in southeast Asia, spread southeast by island-hopping, reached northern or northwestern Sahul sometime between 50,000 and 60,000 years ago, and subsequently spread throughout the continent.

The two populations

In 1973, an article was published in *Nature* by Alan Thorne and Phil Macumber which suggested that 'the late Pleistocene human remains from Kow Swamp display archaic cranial features which suggest the survival of *Homo erectus* in Australia until as recently as 10,000 years ago'.[14] This article sent shivers around the palaeoanthropological world. How dare these two Australian upstarts suggest that the rest of the scientific community had been incorrect in assuming that *Homo erectus* had become extinct several hundred thousand years ago. In fact, Thorne and Macumber were wrong in what they suggested, as they now recognise, because the skulls found at Kow Swamp are clearly *Homo sapiens*, but they are very unusual *Homo sapiens* skulls. They are large, with thick bones, large jaws and teeth, thick brow ridges and sloping foreheads, all characteristics which are common in *Homo erectus* skulls. The Kow Swamp skulls were dated to between 9000 and 13,000 years ago, and there was a statistically valid sample.

Subsequent field work has shown that these 'robust' fossils, as they are generally called, were not just present at Kow Swamp. The nearby site of Cohuna also had robust remains, as did Lake Nitchie and Coobol Creek in New South Wales. Perhaps the most extraordinary find was an undated skull at Cossack, in the northwest of Western Australia, which shared the same features. Whatever these robust fossils represented, they existed on both sides of the continent.[15]

Even more extraordinary was the fact that these skulls were so recent. Evolutionary theory holds that the more 'primitive' characteristics will belong to earlier forms, and the more 'modern' characteristics will belong to the most recent forms. To confuse matters even more, female human remains dated to 25,000 years ago were identified at Lake Mungo. The bones were extremely modern, so much so that they are often referred to as 'gracile'. They have rounded, thin-boned skulls, with small teeth and jaws, no pronounced brow ridges, and fully rounded foreheads. The older population appeared more modern than the younger population. To confuse matters even further, analysis of recent Aboriginal skeletal remains showed enormous variation, but generally not reaching the two extremes found in the robust and gracile fossils.

So what was happening in Australia during the terminal Pleistocene around 10–15,000 years ago? Do we really have two distinct populations living side by side and not interbreeding for more than 30,000 years? Or do we have a great deal of diversity within a single population?

First, it is wise to consider what the biological history of Aboriginal people may have been since they arrived in Australia. There is variation within Aboriginal populations from different parts of the country. In the tropical north, Aboriginal people tend to be tall,

thin and dark, whereas in the south they are shorter and stockier in
stature and lighter in colour. These variations are relatively easy to
explain in terms of adapting to particular climates and environments.
The tall, thin, dark body type is eminently suited to survival in tropical climates, whereas a stockier build and a lighter colour is better
suited for colder climates. The same phenomenon can be seen particularly in European and African human populations. Some of the variation may therefore be ascribed to adaptation to particular environments within Australia over the past 50,000 years.

Indeed, other factors may also be involved. The Tasmanian
Aboriginal population had several characteristics which distinguished it from the adjacent mainland Aboriginal populations in
Victoria, almost certainly due to the fact that the two population had
been isolated physically and genetically for 12,000 years.

It is also worth recognising the fact that the variation which
appears to occur in Pacific Island populations is probably even more
recent. The peopling of the Pacific began around 6000 years ago, yet
there is substantial variation between different Polynesian populations.

Variation caused by geographic separation does not explain what
we observe in the two Aboriginal populations. There were no geographic boundaries between Kow Swamp and Lake Mungo. Indeed, a
major river system linked the two.

There are at least three theories which could account for the fossil evidence:

- There were two waves of colonisation.
- There was enormous variability in a single wave.
- There was selection pressure at work at the end of the
  Pleistocene which favoured people with large teeth and jaws.

Alan Thorne is a strong advocate of the two-wave theory. Indeed
he goes so far as to identify the sources of these two waves. Thorne
argues that the initial colonisation of Australia came from a population which had been derived from the Javan form of *Homo erectus*,
and therefore retained many of the characteristics found in the
Javanese fossils. This robust group spread throughout Australia, and
was followed, perhaps 40,000 years ago, by a second wave of people
who originated not in southeast Asia, but in China. He sees similarities between Chinese fossils dated to around 60,000 years ago and
the gracile Aborigines found at Lake Mungo and elsewhere, and he
believes he can trace these same characteristics back to the Chinese
Homo erectus fossils. Crucial to this argument is acceptance of the
multiregional hypothesis. The other problem with Thorne's argument
is that these two populations remained genetically but not geographi-

cally isolated from each other for 30,000 years, and then interbred completely within the last 9000 years.

The second model suggests that there was enormous variability in the original colonising population, and that the Mungo and Kow Swamp fossils are the two extremes of this continuum. The problem here is that nowhere in modern Aboriginal populations is either extreme common, and there is no obvious reason why such variation should not be reflected in all populations, rather than being seen differently in different geographic areas.

The third model suggests that the robust Kow Swamp fossils were indeed the direct descendants of the gracile Lake Mungo type. It argues that there were strong selection pressures during the terminal Pleistocene, between 18,000 and 10,000 years ago, which may have favoured large jaws and teeth, capable of chewing and breaking down fibrous plant foods, whereas people who were eating fish and mussels at Lake Mungo had no such selection pressures operating on them. The difficulty here is that the Holocene has been stable, so why are not all modern Aboriginal people like the Kow Swamp people? In fact, it has been shown that selection pressures during the Holocene may have favoured Aboriginal people of smaller stature. Peter Brown has suggested that the size of Aboriginal people may have declined by as much as 20% over the last 10,000 years.[16] One consequence would be a corresponding reduction in the size of the teeth, jaws and skull. This could explain why no contemporary Aboriginal populations are as robust as the Kow Swamp fossils.

To confuse matters even further, it has been found that at least some of the Kow Swamp skulls have been artificially deformed: that is, the heads of the babies were flattened to create a sloping forehead, presumably for cultural reasons.[17] This, of course, does not explain all of the differences, and indeed not all of the Kow Swamp fossils are artificially deformed.

Just how different from one another these two populations are is difficult to determine. In general, male human skulls are more robust than female skulls. Kow Swamp, Cohuna, Mossgiel and Lake Nitchie males are all well outside the range for modern males, and indeed Kow Swamp females are outside the female range. At the other end of the scale, the Lake Mungo woman is even more gracile than modern female Aborigines, and the Mungo and Keilor males are more gracile than contemporary male populations.

So it appears that the differences are statistically significant. This can be important if we are trying to understand what impact human populations had on the Australian environment. Did these two populations have different technologies — exploit different resources — have

different population densities — occupy different microhabitats — use
fire in different ways — and therefore impact on the environment in
different ways?

To answer these questions, we must first decide if we accept the
multiregional hypothesis or the out-of-Africa hypothesis, or reject
them both; after all, if *Homo erectus* and *Homo sapiens* are simply
variations within the same species, then the variation we see within
the fossil Aboriginal populations should be of no great surprise,
because it represents variations within a species. Whatever we
decide, we must be aware that there has always been enormous variability in the Australian environment, and possibly in the human
population which occupied that environment. Even Alan Thorne
acknowledges this fact when he states:

> Of course the development of the Australian population was hardly as
> simple or straightforward as that. It was an extremely complex process,
> involving both physical and cultural integration, spread over perhaps
> 50,000 years. It did not consist of two boatloads of different people who
> later intermingled, but an endless series of arrivals at different places
> and from different directions, joining others who had come before and
> scattered across the landscape. We have no way of knowing exactly
> when it began, who came first, or whether there were any large gaps in
> the sequence of arrivals.[18]

Cultural evolution

From the time *Homo habilis* first evolved in Africa, and perhaps even
earlier, human ancestors have been using stone tools. The earliest stone
tools were crude choppers, but by about one million years ago *Homo
erectus* was using a wide range of stone tools, dominated by the characteristic handaxes. Neanderthals had their own characteristic core and
flake tools, and *Homo sapiens sapiens* is often characterised by his
diverse range of specialised flake tools, including many microlithic
tools, and the later appearance of edge-ground tools. However, this is
not a neat sequence. Different tools were used at different times in different parts of the word. It is likely that in the forested parts of southeast Asia, where stone is rare, organic materials like bamboo and shell
were used instead of stone for creating a sharp cutting edge.

The transition from hunting and gathering to agriculture, which
took place in many parts of the world over the last 10,000 years, was
not a step forward in some master evolutionary plan, but a alternative
way of surviving in a harsh environment with a growing human population density. There are many problems which human populations

face when they adopt agriculture. They need to invest a great deal of time and labour in the hope of harvesting a successful crop, and as a result are dependent on a small number of resources. If these resources are no longer available, due to disease, drought or some other problem, then the population may suffer dire consequences.

Yet there is a wide perception that hunter-gatherers — who generally had a better diet, more leisure time, less disease, and in some cases higher population densities over large areas — were at an earlier phase in cultural development. They were not earlier or more primitive — they were just different.

In many aspects, early Aboriginal technology is unique. Aboriginal people made the earliest ocean crossings to colonise a new continent. They lived in Tasmania during the ice ages 20–30,000 years ago, at which time they were the most southerly human population on earth.[19] They were amongst the first people in the world to develop edge-ground axes, which have been found in sites in Arnhem Land dating to more than 20,000 years ago, and perhaps more than 30,000 years ago in north Queensland — which would make them the earliest ground artefacts in the world.[20] However, the archaeological evidence is far from complete. Organic materials preserve poorly in most Australian soils, and there are very few organic remains from any of the early occupation sites. The wide range of wooden artefacts, shell and bone tools, and fibre products which were almost certainly in use 50,000 years ago, have left no trace in the Australian archaeological record. It is clear that the early colonisers had a level of technological sophistication which enabled them to successfully adapt to the Australian environment and spread throughout at least the more favourable parts of the continent.

Spread of population

If we assume that Aboriginal people had reached the northwestern part of Sahul by about 50,000 years ago, how did they go about colonising the remainder of the continent? This process has been a matter of debate amongst the Australian community of prehistorians for the past twenty years. In 1977 Sandra Bowdler suggested that the economy of these early Aborigines was such that they would tend to concentrate on marine and riverine resources, and that the population would have spread along the coast and then up the larger rivers. She believed that non-aquatic adaptations, such as to mountains and deserts, came relatively late in the sequence.[21]

This model contrasts with one which Paul S. Martin proposed for the Americas, and which he believes is valid for Australia. Martin suggests there was an initial point of colonisation somewhere in the northwest part of the continent, and from this point the population spread rapidly across the entire continent, wiping out the Australian megafauna as it went. This model makes the rather bold assumption that *all* the early colonists were primarily big-game hunters.[22] This generalisation may apply for the Americas, where the early stone technology is clearly that of big-game hunters, but it seems less likely for an island continent being colonised by island populations.

Other earlier models, such as one proposed by Joseph Birdsell, predicted that waves of Aborigines could spread across the continent from a small group (say 25 people), and populate the entire area in less than 2,500 years (Birdsell actually came up with the figure 2,204 years).[23]

One of the major criticisms of these models is that there have been major changes in the size and shape of Sahul since the original colonisation. Bowdler argued that the rising sea levels, rather than reducing available land and causing economic pressure, may have actually increased the availability of marine resources by the creation of larger estuaries like Sydney Harbour. She used her research work in Tasmania to show that although there was a significant loss of land when Tasmania was separated from the mainland (about 70% in the immediate region), there was an increase of about 30% in the effective amount of coastline. If the Aborigines had an economy based on marine resources, then the rising sea level may have increased the amount of food resources available and allowed an increase in the population.[24]

On the then available archaeological evidence, Bowdler's argument was strong, and there was and still is a great deal of support for the idea that early Aborigines were essentially coastal people who foraged inland rather than a widespread population using all of the available resources across a range of environments.

The problems with Bowdler's model come with the recent discovery of early sites in the arid regions of Central Australia, and in the mountains away from the coast.[25] There is also archaeological evidence to suggest that the dominant use of specialised fishing equipment like multipronged spears and hooks and lines are a recent development, perhaps less than 3000 years old.[26]

The difficulty in testing Bowdler's model is that if all the early sites were coastal, they are now lying under the oceans which surround Australia, drowned as the sea levels rose after about 15,000 years ago. The sea reached its present level by about 6000 years ago, and from this time on we have large numbers of coastal sites being occupied for the first time.

At the present time the consensus is that the truth probably lies somewhere between the two approaches. It is likely that the coasts were followed initially, but that the population then spread across all favourable environmental zones. Certainly by 20,000 years ago, there are examples of occupation sites found in mountains, deserts and all places in between.

Cultural and biological isolation?

An important question about the Australian human fossils should not be 'was there one stream or many?', but 'if there was only one stream, why?' After all, if people could cross the ocean barriers 50,000 years ago, why did they not continue to do so?

Perhaps we should phrase this question differently. Do we have any firm evidence that there was more than a single migration? For the moment, let us leave aside the question of the robust and gracile fossils and look at other evidence. Are there changes evident in the archaeological record which *must* indicate an outside influence? There is at least one — the arrival of the dingo on the Australian mainland.

The dingo was a relatively late arrival on the scene. The earliest dingo remains are not more than 4000 years old, suggesting that before this time there were no large placental mammals in Australia beside man. The only way a population of dingoes could reach Australia is by being brought in with humans, almost certainly in some kind of boat or canoe. If this is the case, we do have some definite evidence of contact with the outside world. Dogs which may be ancestral to the dingo are found in many places in South-East Asia — in fact some dogs in the Papua-New Guinea highlands are very similar. It is possible that the contact was across Torres Strait, with the contact taking place between mainland Aborigines through Torres Strait Islanders to the New Guinea mainland. Certainly some aspects of New Guinean culture traversed the Torres Strait, including the technology to produce sophisticated dug-out canoes. To the south, canoes were made of sheets of bark, and in some regions there were no canoes at all.[27]

If the dingo arrived via this route, why were other aspects of New Guinean culture not also introduced? Pigs formed an important component of New Guinea culture, but there is no firm date for the introduction of pigs into New Guinea. Bows and arrows were not adopted by Aboriginal people; gardening was not adopted; in fact, the effect of this contact was minimal.

We know from contact history and archaeological excavations that

visitors from the Indonesian port of Macassa made contact with
Aborigines when they sailed south to collect bêche-de-mer, or sea
cucumber. There are nineteenth-century accounts and descriptions of
Macassans off the Kimberley coast, and as far east as Cape York.
They even built processing plants in parts of the Northern Territory
and the Kimberleys, and perhaps took Aboriginal people on their
boats with them. Macknight excavated one of these Macassan sites in
Anuru Bay, where he found the remains of fourteen stone structures.[28]
Similar structures have been found on a small island north of Groote
Eylandt and on Elcho Island. However, their influence on the cultural
traditions was negligible, with the possible exception of the introduction of metal fishhooks, glass for cutting tools, and perhaps pipes for
smoking tobacco. In any event, Macknight believes the contact with
the Macassans did not begin until around AD 1700.

The island of Timor is only 300 km from the Australian coast, so it
is highly likely that over the past 5000 years some ocean voyagers actually reached Australia. From this time onwards the vast expanses of the
Pacific Ocean were being colonised by seafaring people. However, any
outside contacts over the last few thousand years have had little if any
influence on the biological make-up of the Aboriginal people. Although
there may have been contacts with the outside world, the population
appears to have remained essentially genetically isolated.

CHAPTER 3

Adapting to changing environments

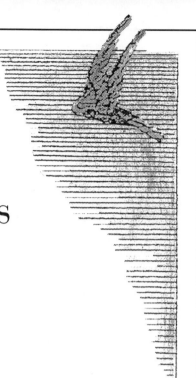

What was Australia like when Aboriginal people arrived 50,000 years ago? Obviously it was much larger than it is today. The coast was anything from ten to several hundred kilometres away from its present position. New Guinea, Kangaroo Island and Tasmania were all joined to Australia, and a broad low plain extended from northern Queensland across to New Guinea.

The vegetation of tropical Sahul was remarkably similar to the vegetation on the islands from which the Aborigines had come. Some estimates suggest that about 80% of the plant species growing along the northern coasts were found on the tropical islands of southeast Asia. If this is the case, and if the people depended largely on marine resources and vegetable foods, then there may have been few problems in simply transposing their culture from southeastern Sunda to northwestern Sahul.

A major difference would have been found with the fauna. Because of the isolation, Australia had evolved a diverse range of marsupials which occupied the same niches as placental animals in other parts of the world. In addition to the species which are still to be found like kangaroos, wallabies, possums and koalas, there were also the large group of animals referred to collectively as the Australian megafauna.

The other important aspect of the environment is climate, particularly temperature and rainfall. The obvious effect of the Ice Ages was that the temperature was colder, and in different parts of Australia this has been shown to vary both spatially and temporally. It seems that the average temperatures during the periods of extreme low sea level fell by somewhere between 4 and 7 degrees Celsius, while the rainfall may have decreased by as much as 50%. The implications for such changes are clear. The lush forests would be reduced, and many areas in the south of the continent would become grasslands and open woodlands. Parts of southeastern Australia and Tasmania became glaciated. This would have consequences for the fauna, and although there is no clear evidence that a reduction in the number of species was caused by the changing climate, it is clear that there was a decline in the number of species, and by 15,000 years ago most of the Australian megafauna had disappeared. One possible explanation is that if large animals were dependent on the availability of water, then the cold, dry, windy conditions which prevailed between about 25,000 and 15,000 years ago would have been totally unsuitable for them.

There is clear evidence of major climatic changes across Australia over the period of human occupation. This evidence is derived from a variety of sources and by a range of methods. The greatest period of aridity corresponded to the lowest sea level, and this occurred around 18,000 years ago. At this time the coldest conditions existed, with glaciation in Tasmania, aridity and lunette-building of the Willandra Lakes system, and apparent abandonment of many areas in Central Australia.[1] At the same time other sites are being occupied for the first time. Why do these changes in settlement pattern occur, and were there technological or social adaptations which correspond to these time periods?

By around 6000 years ago, the sea levels had stabilised around their present levels, and again we find large numbers of sites, particularly coastal sites, being occupied for the first time. However, even within this period of stable mid–late Holocene sea levels, there are suggestions that perhaps two distinct stages of occupation occurred, one around 4000 years ago and another around 1500 years ago.

It is clear that Aboriginal people responded to the changing climate by changing their spatial distribution across the landscape and by modifying their technology to exploit new resources. It is possible to detect changes in the archaeological record which might explain how Aboriginal people coped with these changing environments. To do this, it is necessary to investigate the changes in Aboriginal settlement patterns and technology in those areas which are likely to be most sensitive to climatic change — places which still have cold climates like Tasmania, the Blue Mountains and the Southern Highlands of New South Wales; places which were impacted by changing sea levels like the southeast coastal strip; and places which became inhospitable because of increasing aridity, like the Willandra Lakes system and the Central Australian deserts. Each of these regions, at various times and in its own way, can be described as an environmentally sensitive zone.

Tasmania

The earliest occupation sites in Tasmania are more than 30,000 years old.[2] By 18,000 years ago, much of Tasmania, around 5000 square km, was covered with glacial ice, and other areas were strongly affected by periglacial conditions. Although a few Aboriginal sites like Cave Bay Cave on Hunter Island were occupied, there is little evidence from the inland areas of Tasmania, and none at all from what was the coastline, all possible sites now having been submerged by rising sea levels.[3] Certainly all the sites known from this period are characterised by few stone artefacts which are similar in nature to the mainland stone industry, and most but not all of the fauna being exploited is essentially modern. Many of the sites in the southeast, where hunters had exploited wallabies between 25,000 and 20,000 years ago, had been abandoned and Tasmania appears to have supported a very small Aboriginal population.

There are a few sites which were first occupied between 20,000 and 16,000 years ago, one of which is possibly the richest archaeological site in Australia. Kutikina dates from 19,000 years ago, and in less than one cubic metre of deposit there were recovered over 250,000 animal bones and over 40,000 stone artefacts.[4] At Bone Cave, which dates from around 16,000 years ago, there was a clear emphasis on hunting red-necked wallabies, and there is also evidence of skin cloaks being worn. Bone points are found in these deposits.[5]

Between 18,000 and 12,000 years ago, sea levels rose and the climate became warmer. As a result, Tasmania became an island, totally separated from the mainland by Bass Strait. This isolated the Tasmanians from the outside world for the next 12,000 years. Small populations remained on the larger Bass Strait Islands, but eventually these died out, and the isolation became complete until Europeans arrived in the eighteenth century.

There are few archaeological sites in Tasmania which appear to have evidence of occupation between 14,000 and 8000 years ago. There are two points of view about what happened in Tasmania following the separation from the mainland. Rhys Jones has argued the following:

Perhaps the culture, remote for thousands of years from any outside stimulus, was becoming simplified and losing some of its 'useful arts'. Perhaps in the very long run... 3000 people were not enough to support and maintain a culture even of a simplicity of that practised during late Pleistocene Australia.[6]

Many other prehistorians see Tasmanian prehistory certainly in terms of change and adaptation, but not of degeneration. It is clear that by around 8000 years ago many near coastal-sites were being occupied for the first time, and all of the sites which had formerly existed in the southwest of the island were long abandoned to the dense rainforests.

Probably the best known of these coastal sites is at Rocky Cape, and it was Rhys Jones who carried out this excavation.[7] The stone tools changed little over time, and were all scrapers. The fauna consisted of marine and terrestrial resources, including seal, wallabies and bandicoots. Two types of food did demonstrate significant change over time. In the lower units dating between 8000 and 4000 years ago, parrot fishes were common. In the upper units all fish remains disappeared entirely. In the lower units there were few bird remains, but in the upper units birds, particularly shags, were common. Shellfish formed a major component of the diet throughout the occupation of the site, although there appear to have been changes over time in the proportions of different species. The absence of fish seems to be related to an increase in the exploitation of land animals in the upper units.

Bone points were found in the lower units, but not in the upper units. They were made from marsupial long bones and form a significant proportion of the marsupial remains from the lower units.

At least some of the stone used in the upper levels seems to have been obtained from some distance away, suggesting movement of populations or perhaps trade. There seems to be a more efficient use of the stone tools, with increasing numbers of working edges per tool and a greater ratio of tools to waste. This corresponds to an increase in the number of land animals from the site, and this correlation between obtaining raw materials from a greater distance and greater exploitation of land animals has led Peter White to suggest that this may have been the time when the Tasmanians first began to use fire to regularly burn the underbrush, permitting greater movement and increased availability of terrestrial animals.[8]

Many other Tasmanian coastal sites were first occupied in the last 2–3000 years, and some of these suggest seasonal occupation. At most sites, the fauna are essentially marine, with some sites being interpreted as summer seal-hunting camps. At Cave Bay Cave on Hunter Island, the last stage of occupation dates from around 2300 years ago and the faunal assemblage is dominated by shellfish, rats and birds. As in all late Tasmanian sites, there is no evidence of bony fish having been eaten. The birds appear to suggest a summer occupation.[9]

On the southwest coast, Ron Vanderwal also found evidence to suggest seasonal hunting of seals on the off-shore islands, and he proposed that the development of canoes at this time could explain his results. He also suggests that there was a significant increase in the Tasmanian population within the last 2000 years.[10]

Whatever they were hunting and eating, the Tasmanian Aborigines 3000 years ago did not have a number of technological specialisations which were present on the mainland. The did not have spearthrowers, boomerangs, edge-ground axes, pronged or barbed fishing spears, hafted adze flakes, nets, traps, sewn cloaks, and they did not have the dingo. All of their stone artefacts were held in the hand. Yet they survived quite well, and seem to have been admirably adapted to exploit their environment, certainly using a relatively simple technology, but apparently using it quite effectively. The change in resource base and greater use of fire appears to occur within the last few thousand years.[11] Perhaps Tasmania provides some insight into the strategies which were adopted on the mainland to cope with changing climate — abandonment of some areas during difficult times, and reoccupation and technological specialisation during favourable periods.

Clearly there were also major changes taking place in the late Holocene period, when the climate was stable. This also has its parallels on the mainland.

The Blue Mountains

The same problems which were encountered by Aboriginal people in the southwest of Tasmania might also be found in the upper reaches of the Blue Mountains of southeastern Australia. At the present time there is no evidence for Aboriginal occupation earlier than 20,000 years for the upper mountains. There is one site at Kings Tableland, west of Sydney, where a few stone flakes were found in a deposit dated to 22,000 years, but there is a marked disconformity in the deposition of sediments within this site immediately above the flakes, and the early dating of the site is not totally secure. The earliest securely dated sites in the Blue Mountains are at Lyre Bird Dell near Leura, where a large rock shelter was first occupied 12,000 years ago. Although it was originally suggested that this site was then abandoned, several backed blades indicative of a late Holocene period of occupation have been found on the floor of this shelter, demonstrating that it was in use more recently. However, there may well have been a period of abandonment.[12]

At Shaw's Creek, right at the foot of the mountains, a large rock shelter shows continuous but initially low-intensity occupation from 15,000 years ago, probably continuing to the ethnographic present.[13] This site should not be considered a mountain site, as it is only fourteen metres above sea level, but it clearly establishes that Aboriginal people were present in the vicinity of the mountains. Nearby, there is also a 28,000 year date for the Cranebrook Terrace, which is also at the foot of the mountains.[14] A suggested date of 45,000 years for stone artefacts in the Cranebrook Terrace now seems unlikely.[15]

The majority of sites in the Blue Mountains date from the last 5000 years, and most are less than 3000 years old. On the western side of the mountains, sites in the Capertee Valley were first used around 8000 years ago, and there is no evidence for earlier occupation in this region.[16]

The picture of Aboriginal settlement is that in the upper mountains there was little if any occupation much before 12,000 years ago, but by that time, and a little earlier at Shaw's Creek right at the foot of the escarpment, Aborigines had begun to exploit the cooler environments, perhaps as seasonal visits during the summer. Once the major climatic and technological changes of the mid-Holocene had been accomplished, settlement spread up into the mountains and many new sites were occupied for the first time.

The Southern Highlands

Of fourteen sites excavated in the Southern Highlands by Josephine Flood, only two show evidence of occupation prior to the last 4000 years.[17] At Clogg's Cave, bones and artefacts dating from between 18,000 and 13,500 years ago have been found in a relatively cold environment. Why should this site first be occupied at the height of the glacial maximum, when conditions were at their coldest and driest? Perhaps we should look to Tasmania for the answer. Did the inhabitants of Tasmania 23–20,000 years ago exploit an environment which was duplicated further north as the temperatures dropped? Are we actually looking at a cold-adapted economy? Josephine Flood actually suggests that the site was occupied in the winter on the basis of the absence of freshwater mussels. She speculates the water of the rivers would have been too cold to collect this resource.

The fauna in the site was diverse and included possums, macropods, koalas, wombats and bandicoots. Clearly the economy was based on the exploitation of terrestrial animals which were essentially modern and the parallels with Tasmania are apparent.

Another site in the Southern Highlands is Birrigai, close to Tidbinbilla and the Murrumbidgee River. This is dated to 21,000 years ago, but the numbers of artefacts are small (a total of 69, most of which came from the last 2000 years). No faunal remains were recovered from the early layers, and little can be said except that Aboriginal people were using this area sporadically from around 21,000 years ago.[18]

One of the big attractions of the Southern Highlands for Aboriginal people over the past few thousand years has been the annual summer swarming of the bogong moth. This event attracted Aborigines from a considerable distance and they spent a fruitful time eating the fat moths. This activity suggests that extended social networks had developed by the late Holocene. However, there is no archaeological evidence to indicate that bogong moth exploitation was anything other than a late development specific to the Southern Highlands.

Southeast coasts

At around the same time that Clogg's Cave was first occupied 18,000 years ago, two other sites on the coast of New South Wales were also being used by Aboriginal people. These sites are Bass Point south of Wollongong, and Burrill Lake near Bateman's Bay.[19] Both sites were first investigated because there was a shell midden at or near the surface. Both occur adjacent to the present coastline, but at the time of the first occupation they would have both been approximately 15 km away from the coast, overlooking river valleys. Bass Point is an open site; Burrill Lake is a rock shelter. Burill Lake was first occupied 20,000 years ago, while the earliest date for Bass Point is 18,000 years ago. After periods of abandonment, both sites were again used when the sea levels stabilised. There is no evidence for the fauna being exploited at this early period of occupation, but whatever it was it almost certainly wasn't marine.

With over 60 sites investigated and carbon-dated, all other sites so far excavated on the south coast of New South Wales date from after 8000 years ago when the sea level had risen, and the vast majority date from the last 3000 years. It seems there was a surge of activity at a time when environmental conditions were at their worst, followed by abandonment and later occupation when the sea levels have risen and stabilised, at which time marine resources were being exploited.

The Willandra Lakes system

The sand dunes of Lake Mungo in western New South Wales have provided evidence of Aboriginal occupation extending back at least
35,000 years, and these sites are now recognised as being a significant
part of the world's prehistoric heritage. The Willandra Lakes are now
given the status of being on the World Heritage listing. Mungo is part
of a network of lakes which have not filled in the past 10,000 years,
but between 35,000 and about 15,000 years ago they were subjected
to periodic filling and emptying. In the dry periods, sand dunes
(lunettes, because of their crescent shape) were built up on the eastern
side of the lakes. These became the camp sites for Aboriginal people
when the lakes filled. The reasons why the lakes filled are complicat-
ed, by the major contributing factors appear to have been an increased
rainfall in the catchment area (or perhaps rapid melting of glaciers)
and the lower evaporation due to colder climate and less wind.[20]

The archaeological sites around Lake Mungo consist mainly of
hearths and scatters of stone and faunal remains. The fauna have been
identified as essentially modern, and include fish and freshwater mussels from the lake, and mammals and emu eggs from the surrounding
area. The kind of information which can be obtained from such data
can be important. For instance, it was possible to suggest that the fish
were being netted, rather than being speared, because all the fish of
one species (golden perch) were juveniles of the same size, the kind of
distribution which would result from netting but not from spearing.[21]

One interesting change which occurred after about 18,000 years
ago was the presence of grinding stones in the area, unknown until this
time. The grinding stones were used for grinding seeds of the panicum
grass into cakes to be baked. The panicum is common in drier environments, so when the environment changed it seems that a new technology was used to exploit the new resource. There is still some doubt, however, as to whether these grindstones were actually used for seeds.[22]

The evidence for Aboriginal occupation of the Lake Mungo area
following the drying-out of the lakes in the late Pleistocene is scarce,
but some sites have been recorded on the floor of the dry lake which
clearly belong to the late Holocene period, once again suggesting a
more recent use of the area based on the exploitation of non-aquatic
resources.

Deserts

The discovery that several sites in Central Australia were occupied
prior to 18,000 years ago demonstrated that areas which are now arid
may have been more attractive to Aboriginal people in the past. Smith

and Veth have both proposed models for Aboriginal land use in the arid zone, and they suggest that the data indicate abandonment of marginal areas when conditions deteriorated.[23] However, the first occupation of Puritjarra rock shelter in the Northern Territory is around 23,000 years ago; Colless Creek in Queensland is at 19,000 years ago; Miriwun on the Ord River in Western Australia is at 18,000 years ago; Quininup in southwestern Western Australia at 18,000 years ago; and many other sites around the same time, when conditions were deteriorating — or were they?[24] Faunal evidence from Miriwun suggests that the same resources were being used during this early phase of occupation as were used in the later Holocene phases.[25] In other words, the environment has not changed dramatically in the past 18,000 years, even if it was a little drier then.

One particular stone tool type, tula adze flakes, is first found in the early levels of Miriwun, and they also occur in Pleistocene levels at Quininup Brook. Peter Veth suggests it was the adoption of these adzes which allowed the Holocene exploitation of the desert resources, yet here we have the same desert tools recorded in two semi-arid zones 12,000 years earlier.[26]

Australia-wide adaption at the glacial maximum

The trends across the continent were not uniform, and while rainfall could be decreasing in some areas it may have been increasing in others. In Tasmania, we find abandonment of large areas at the time of glacial maximum, and shortly after we find the first occupation of similar environments further north in Victoria and in New South Wales. There are no data on coastal populations, but it must be assumed they remained on the coast, presumably retaining their coastal technology and economy. When the sea levels stabilised, we find coastal sites begin to be used in Tasmania. After around 4000 years ago, there appear to be major changes in the technology and economy, perhaps associated with greater trading networks or larger seasonal movements of population, perhaps corresponding to greater reliance on seals and terrestrial resources.

The Blue Mountains were used only sporadically before 12,000 years ago, and then only rarely until the last 4000 years ago, when many sites were first occupied by people using the new microlithic technology.

In western New South Wales the abandonment of the then-dry Willandra Lakes system was taking place, yet at the same time many semi-arid areas were first occupied in the 'corridors' proposed by Peter Veth.[27]

There appear to be a number of processes happening at the same time at around 18,000 years ago. Some areas were abandoned, and others were occupied for the first time, including many semi-arid zones which were previously not used or little used. In some areas we must assume a continuation of an economy which remained unchanged — for example, along the coast where the concept of 'coastal adaptation' could well apply.

By 8000 years ago when the sea approached the present levels, we find increasing numbers of sites occupied for the first time or, in the case of Burrill Lake and Bass Point, reoccupied. Then around 5–4000 years ago, there were major shifts in settlement pattern — new sites along the coast, in the mountains, on the plains and along the rivers. This was followed by a period of rapid technological change, social change and changing patterns of resource exploitation.

These shifts in Aboriginal settlement pattern could have occurred because the distribution of animals changed, or because the people changed, or perhaps because the vegetation had changed in response to Aboriginal burning. Although the changes which can be observed in the archaeological record may well represent Aboriginal people moving and adapting to changing environments, they may also be explained by factors like changed site usage and variations in archaeological visibility.

Aboriginal people had two options when climatic conditions worsened — abandon the area and move on to a new one while continuing to exploit the same resource base, or adopt a new technology and exploit a different range of resources. For the Pleistocene, it seems that the former strategy was largely adopted, but during the late Holocene, technological change and exploitation of new resources was the preferred option, and possibly the only one.

On this basis, it seems likely that Aboriginal environmental impacts during the Pleistocene are less likely to have played a significant role in the distribution of plants and animals than climate change, whereas during the relative climatic stability of the Holocene, with the adoption of a range of new technologies and the exploitation of a wider range of resources, Aboriginal people may well have had a more dramatic impact. Certainly, in the warmer conditions of the Holocene, Aboriginal burning may have had a much greater effect than at any other time in the past.

CHAPTER 4

Fire and Australian vegetation

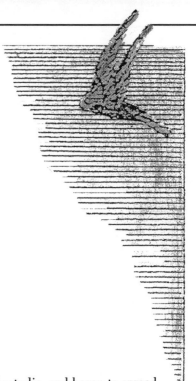

Once Aboriginal people arrived in Australia, and began to spread across the continent, did they have any significant impact on the Australian environment? Did they effect the distribution of plants and animals across the landscape, particularly though their use of fire? This is a complex issue, and a number of researchers have approached this question from different perspectives.

There are two camps of people who have diametrically opposite views on this question. David Horton suggests that: 'Aboriginal use of fire had little impact on the environment and... the patterns of distribution of plants and animals which obtained 200 years ago would have been essentially the same whether or not Aborigines had previously been living here.'[1] Taking the extreme position — little or no human impact — Horton believes that it was climatic change which was the driving force behind the development of contemporary Australian vegetation patterns. Consequently, since the Holocene period has been relatively stable, he must also argue that these changes were virtually completed by 10,000 years ago. Yet there is evidence for some important changes in the vegetation during the Holocene.

At the other end of the spectrum, Gurdip Singh argued that changes in the vegetation around Lake George, near Canberra, were caused by Aboriginal burning, and he argued that these changes began around 120,000 years ago. His view was that Aborigines first arrived in Australia at that time.[2] Such an early date has been supported by recent evidence from deep-sea cores off the Queensland coast.[3] Horton argues that fire has always been a component of Australian ecosystems and Aborigines had no impact; Singh argues that fire only became important with the advent of the Aborigines. The truth probably lies somewhere between these two extreme views.

There are a number of important questions which need to be answered about Aboriginal burning practices. How long have Aborigines been burning intensively? What does this burning do to the vegetation, and as a consequence to the fauna? Can we detect evidence of Aboriginal burning in the archaeological record? Robyn Clark believes that, on the basis of the evidence:

> Aborigines neither created nor maintained vast areas of grassland, although their burning may have been responsible for the continuation of patches of grassland or woodland within larger forested regions. Climate has been and is far more important than fire in determining the distribution of Australian vegetation, but Aboriginal burning might have effected the rate of vegetation change.[4]

This discussion begs another question — were Aboriginal burning methods always the same? The use of the ethnographic analogy — making the assumption that what we see in the ethnographic present is the same as what existed in the prehistoric past — is fraught with danger. The same cautious approach which is used by prehistorians in assessing artefact functions or cultural practices should be used when investigating Aboriginal burning practices.

In some situations, the evidence suggests that the Aboriginal use of resources which were increased by regular burning is a relatively recent event. Beaton has studied the Aboriginal use of cycads, a group of plants which contain highly toxic compounds.[5] He documents increases in the number of edible cones after firing and suggests that one of the uses of fire was to increase the yield of these plants. He also believes that they were first exploited around 4000 years ago when the technological processing to remove the poisonous components became known to Aboriginal people. Again we have this critical period of around 4000 years ago, when major technological changes are evident in the archaeological record.

Palynology

The techniques Singh and other researchers have used to recreate past vegetation associations are those of palynology, the study of fossil pollen. Pollen and charcoal particles are generally preserved in the sediments at the bottom of lakes or bogs. The Lake George pollen sequence extends back over 350,000 years and the core is almost 9 metres deep. Peter Kershaw's Lynch's Crater site in northern Queensland goes back 190,000 years.[6] The earlier dates are correlated with oxygen isotope studies of ocean temperatures, which reflect the variations in climate during the Pleistocene over the last 2 million years or so.

Lake George has an interesting history. It last filled to overflowing sometime between 19,000 and 26,000 years ago. In the last 200 years it has varied between being completely dry and containing water to a depth of 7.5 metres. The vegetation around Lake George today is closely linked with the climate and rainfall, and not so much with the soil or rock type. The vegetation consists of low open forests, open woodlands and grasslands. In the eucalypt-dominated forests and woodlands, *Acacia* and *Exocarpus*, the native cherry, are common. The higher mountain ranges around Lake George support tall open (wet-sclerophyll) forests.

A pollen core is generally divided into a number of zones, based on the frequency of particular types of pollen. The Lake George core was divided into eleven zones. In some of these zones, grass pollen dominated, and shrub and tree pollen was limited. These periods correspond to cooler climatic conditions, which favour grasses over woody vegetation. Warm conditions are represented by the high proportion of sclerophyll taxa such as eucalypts. In the periods of grasses and cool conditions, counts of charcoal particles are low.

During the warm interglacial periods before Aborigines had arrived in Australia, the surrounding forests were dominated by *Casuarina* and *Podocarpus*. There were small numbers of eucalypts and other myrtaceous taxa, and when these increased, so did the charcoal count. In Zone F, which is believed to date to around 120,000 years ago (although Wright has suggested that it may be much younger), open sclerophyll woodlands, similar to the present vegetation, was present around the lake.[7] Charcoal counts rose to their highest level, and *Casuarina* counts were low. From that time, the grasses and chenopods remained abundant. Singh argued that 'the activity of fires had increased during the last interglacial as compared with the earlier interglacials, a feature which may have been associated with the arrival of Man at Lake George, since the changes in climate alone could not explain the changes in the vegetation'.[8]

As the temperatures cooled during the last glacial maximum, the Casuarina increased and the charcoal counts dropped, but Singh suggests that Aboriginal burning continued right through to the Holocene. It is during the Holocene, the last 10,000 years, that the cool, temperate taxa disappear altogether from the Lake George area. The *Podocarpus* and the tree-fern pollen are no longer found, and within the last 5000 years eucalypts increase dramatically, as does the charcoal count. The vegetation changes from tall to low open forest, and Singh once again argues that the continual Aboriginal burning may have caused this. What he fails to say is that between 10,000 years ago and around 5000 years ago, when the climate is supposedly stable, eucalypts and myrtaceous plants are poorly represented in the core, and these groups and charcoal only increase dramatically over the last 5000 years.

At Lynch's Crater, on the Atherton Tableland, a similar picture emerges, except that the first massive increase in charcoal occurs around 38,000 years ago. Between this time and 26,000 years ago the auracarian forest were replaced by *Casuarina* and *Eucalyptus*. During the Holocene, from around 5000 years ago, rainforests return, but this time they are dominated by angiosperms, not gymnosperms. Charcoal levels, which were low 7000 years ago, increase dramatically around 5000 years ago. In the last few thousand years there has been a reduction in the rainforest and an increase in eucalypts and *Casuarina*.[9]

In these two cases, each author argues that the increase in charcoal can be explained by the arrival of man. However, the increase in charcoal at other sites is explained by the absence of man!

Lashmar's Lagoon is at the extreme eastern end of Kangaroo Island. Radiocarbon dates suggest that the island was occupied from at least 16,000 years ago until at least around 4300 years ago, based on radiocarbon dates of prehistoric sites. The pollen core extends over the last 7000 years, and shows a remarkable change around 2500 years ago, with charcoal increasing dramatically at this time, and *Eucalyptus* replacing *Casuarina*. Robin Clark, who worked on this site, suggests that this change came about because Aborigines stopped regular low-intensity burning, leading to an accumulation of fuel, which then burnt less frequently but more intensively, resulting in the replacement of the *Casuarina* by eucalypts. To support this view, Clark shows that once Europeans occupied the landscape and began burning, the charcoal concentration decreased again! Between 4300 and 2500 years ago, *Acacia* pollen is common, suggesting disturbance and recolonisation. It is interesting to note that Clark believes 'the marked change in burning regime 2500 years ago had little or no long-term effect on the vegetation. Perhaps this is to be expected in a vegetation which is already fire adapted.'[10]

Here we have yet another interpretation of Aboriginal burning. When it stops, charcoal increases, but the vegetation doesn't change because it is already fire-adapted.

Clearly there are several different points of view and different interpretations of essentially the same data. Lesley Head argues that the vegetation associations which will change with increased Aboriginal burning are those which are not fire-adapted, and she points to the differences in vegetation associations across the country. With such variation, it would be unusual if there weren't variations in the response of vegetation to fire. She criticises Singh's data on the basis of the very small pollen counts before 130,000 years ago and suggests the possibility that the older charcoal particles may have been destroyed. In some levels, the pollen counts are too small to make valid statistical comparisons.[11] Richard Wright has suggested that, based on accumulation rates and other sites, Singh's Zone F is not 120,000 years old, but more like 60,000 years old.[12] Horton, among others, has challenged Singh's view that *Casuarina* is a fire-sensitive plant.[13] Clark goes so far as to suggest that, at least as far as Lake George is concerned, Singh's data allows 'nothing to be said with certainty about fire history'. Head, however, does accept Kershaw's suggestion that Aboriginal burning began at Lynch's Crater at 38,000 years ago.

The Tasmanian data presents us with an interesting set of problems. Aboriginal burning seems to have occurred in the southwest during the terminal Pleistocene, perhaps between 18,000 and 12,000 years ago. With the greater rainfall of the Holocene, rainforests developed, probably because of the wetter conditions. Fire was acting in opposition to the direction of climatic change — burning favours sclerophyll vegetation — while the moister climate favoured rainforest plants. Climate won. The same may be said of Lynch's Crater, where rainforests returned. Perhaps what we are observing is the struggle between anthropogenic fires and climate, with climate seeming to come out in front in most situations.[14]

However, there are other forms of evidence which support late Holocene Aboriginal burning as being an important component in determining the vegetation associations, at least in eastern Australia. Hughes and Sullivan have argued that the increase in valley fills in eastern Australia during the last 3000 years was caused by increased Aboriginal burning. Fires removed the groundcover and understorey, and allowed the sandstone slopes to erode more rapidly, filling up the valley floors with deposit.[15] Hickin and Page reported that valley fills from the Wollombi valley had been dated to the last 4000 years, and they published this as a partial retraction of their previous view that valley fills were related to sea level change.[16] Clearly these recent dates for valley fills in the Sydney region indicate some kind of geomorphic process initiated by something other than climate. Hughes and Sullivan point the finger at Aboriginal burning, and it is difficult to find any other satisfactory explanation, although there are other interpretations of the data.

Palynological studies and vegetation analyses in the Sydney region also suggest an increase in Aboriginal burning during the late Holocene. Clark and McLoughlin have found evidence for regular Aboriginal burning in the Lane Cove River Valley, based on charcoal in sediments and the patterns of vegetation, and even suggest that different burning regimes were evident on the shale and sandstone.[17] Kodela and Dodson found evidence for an increase in charcoal associated with a high concentration of eucalypt pollen 3000 years ago in Kuring-gai Chase.[18]

Head points out that in recent times, contemporary Aboriginal groups have been maintaining both fire-dependent and fire-resistant communities. Indeed, what Aboriginal people were trying to achieve was a balance between the need to burn some areas to promote certain resources, and the need to protect other areas where particular plant foods grew, including areas like rainforests and wet sclerophyll forests. Aboriginal burning often produced a mosaic of vegetation associations, maximising the productivity of an area. Rather than suggesting that Aborigines burned the landscape, perhaps it is better to say that they managed the landscape, and that fire was one of the tools which they used.

Rhys Jones was the one of the first to suggest that this burning was controlled or directed.[19] He saw fire as an important tool in increasing the productivity of the land, by replacing mature forests with open woodlands and grasslands. It is probably better to argue that Aborigines contributed little to this process until the late Holocene, when their increased population and more intensive use of fire promoted certain species to the disadvantage of others, but generally on a local scale. Before this time, the direction and extent of vegetation change was largely directed by climate.

The increase in Aboriginal burning was probably a consequence of the introduction or invention of new technologies which allowed Aboriginal people to concentrate on those large resources which were previously so difficult to capture — kangaroos and large wallabies. Fire was initially used to promote and retain the environments which were most suitable for these animals, and fire was subsequently used for maximising the productivity of these areas after the massive Aboriginal population increase which occurred largely because of the greater access to this abundant resource.

However, to suggest that it was Aboriginal burning which caused the sclerophyllous vegetation to flourish is to miss the point.

- Drying out caused selection for vegetation which could survive drought.
- Dry conditions induce fires.
- Vegetation which can survive fire is favoured.
- Climatic fluctuations during the last 50,000 years have resulted in changes in the vegetation.
- Accompanying these changes came associated changes in charcoal concentrations — sometimes greater, sometimes less, depending on the particular environment.
- Only during the late Holocene is the evidence strong for Aboriginal burning having a significant impact on the vegetation associations.
- Once Aboriginal burning stopped, the new European burning regime promoted different vegetation associations, with differing fire frequencies and charcoal production.

When Europeans first settled in Australia in 1788, they found a landscape dominated by eucalypts. Certainly there were some areas of dense vegetation which contained a greater diversity of trees. However, the dominant feature of the landscape was the ubiquitous gum tree. When expeditions began exploring the countryside around Sydney, they encountered a range of vegetation associations very different from those which we see in the National Parks around Sydney today. On soils derived from Hawkesbury sandstone, Wianamatta shale, Tertiary alluvial deposits and igneous intrusions they found environments which reminded them of the manicured parks of England, with trees well spaced and a grassy understorey. Peter Cunningham described the country west of Parramatta and Liverpool as 'a fine timbered country, perfectly clear of bush, through which you might, generally speaking, drive a gig in all directions, without any impediment in the shape of rocks, scrubs, or close forest'.[20] This confirmed earlier accounts by Governor Phillip, who suggested that the trees were 'growing at a distance of some twenty to forty feet from each other, and in general entirely free from brushwood... '[21]

It is clear that it was primarily Aboriginal burning practices which maintained an open environment dominated by well-spaced trees and grass. Once the Aborigines stopped burning, underbrush grew where none had previously existed. Benson and Howell suggest that the growth of the woody weed *Bursaria spinosa* in the Sydney area in the 1820s was probably related to a changed fire regime with the cessation of Aboriginal burning.[22]

While Aboriginal people used fire as a tool for increasing the productivity of their environment, Europeans saw fire as a threat. Without regular low-intensity burning, leaf litter accumulates and crown fires can result, destroying everything in their path. European settlers feared fire, for it could destroy their houses, their crops, and it could destroy them. Yet the environment which was so attractive to them was created by fire. Indeed, it has been suggested that the European settlement of Tasmania followed almost exactly those areas which the Tasmanian Aborigines had regularly burned.[23]

As European settlement spread out from Sydney, traditional Aboriginal burning practices ceased. Once this happened, vegetation associations changed, animals which were once common rapidly declined, and in some cases disappeared altogether. In the more remote areas, this process took longer. In western New South Wales it happened in the 1840s and 1850s. In parts of Central Australia, the extinctions and declines still continue, although other factors are now involved. However, it can be argued that many of these changes are the result of changed fire regimes. Certainly some of the extinctions of the smaller terrestrial mammals in arid Australia occurred long before the introduction of competitors such as the rabbit and predators like the fox and cat.

So, did Aborigines have an important role to play in Australian vegetation? In the long term, probably not; in the last 5000 years, almost certainly, at least in some areas where the Aboriginal population was relatively large, creating a mosaic of vegetation associations. In the last 200 years, Europeans have created a different mosaic of environments, using the far wider range of tools they have had at their disposal.

CHAPTER 5

The extinction of the megafauna

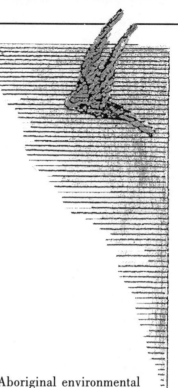

The most vexing question concerning Aboriginal environmental impacts in Australia relates to the extinction of the megafauna, and whether Aborigines were directly or indirectly involved in the extinction process. It is possible that Aborigines hunted them to extinction? Perhaps they modified the landscape with fire to the extent that the megafauna could not survive, or they may have had no impact at all, and the extinctions may have been entirely due to climate change.

In trying to unravel the factors which led to megafaunal extinctions, we are faced with several major difficulties. The biggest problem lies with the dating of the various extinctions. Another relates to the use of the ethnographic analogy. We have few modern analogies which can be used for comparison with the events which took place during the late Pleistocene. Not only do we not know the distribution or population density of people and animals across the landscape during the Pleistocene, but we do not know how or even if Aborigines hunted the megafauna. We do not know how fire was used, or, indeed, if fire was used at all as a Pleistocene land-management tool. We do not know what technology was needed to hunt and kill the large animals.

There is still some doubt if indeed the megafauna all became extinct. There are many zoologists who suggest that at least some of them did not, and that some species of extant large macropods are the descendants of megafauna like *Macropus titan* — they did not become extinct, they merely became more reduced in size, or dwarfed. There are sound reasons for making such a suggestion, because a number of instances have been recorded in the literature where Pleistocene species have become dwarfed.[1]

However, it is clear that many large species did become extinct — animals like *Procoptodon*, *Diprotodon*, *Protemnodon*, *Sthenurus*, *Zygomaturus* and the marsupial lion, *Thylacoleo*. At about the same time as these mammals were becoming extinct, several large birds and reptiles also become extinct. A wide range of large animals, mainly herbivores but including some carnivores, from a range of environmental zones, apparently abundant at the time Aborigines arrived, had died out by the time Europeans arrived in Australia. There are several theories which attempt to explain how and why this occurred.

Technological specialisation

Before venturing into the dilemma of megafaunal extinctions, it is sensible to consider if there is any direct evidence which supports the view that Aborigines hunted or butchered large animals. One Aboriginal stone tool assemblage which, it has been suggested, may have some links with the megafauna, is the Kartan. The Kartan industry consists of heavy core tools and pebble choppers, and is found on Kangaroo Island (whose local name was Karta), the adjacent parts of the South Australian coast, the Flinders Ranges, and more recently at Lime Springs in eastern New South Wales.[2] Nowhere in South Australia is it dated directly. However it is not found in rock shelters, only on open sites.

The Kartan industry consists almost exclusively of large core tools, unifacially flaked pebble tools and hammerstones. There are few flake tools found in Kartan assemblages. Draper believes he has excavated the missing flake component of the Kartan at Cape du Couedic on Kangaroo Island, and the site dates from 7000 years ago. The odd Kartan-like tool which was found in this site was a chopper which may well have been used to butcher sea lions.[3]

At Lime Springs, the Kartan industry was found above an earlier flake assemblage and is associated with megafauna. At Trinkey, Kartan artefacts are associated with *Diprotodon* remains as recently as 7000 years ago.[4] It is possible to speculate that the Kartan was an industry of curated tools used at specific activity sites to butcher large game animals like megafauna or sea lions. If this is so, it will not be found in rock shelters, but only on open sites in environments where seals or megafauna would have been found. The Kartan on Kangaroo Island is restricted to the banks of swamps, lagoons, beaches and rivers, exactly the kinds of environments one might expect to find large game. Analysis of residues on the Kartan artifacts may provide answers to these questions concerning the function of the Kartan stone tools.

Even if there does prove to be a link between the Kartan industry and the butchering of large game, there is very little evidence which indicates the megafauna were actively hunted. Regardless of which model of colonisation is correct, Aborigines had occupied the entire continent by 25,000 years ago, at least in all the favoured environments. At that time they were presumably using resources along the coastal strip; they were exploiting freshwater resources in western New South Wales until the lakes dried out; they were hunting wallabies on the cold grasslands of southwestern Tasmania; and they were probably eating and possibly hunting megafauna everywhere but in the arid centre. The technological traditions are few — most sites are dominated by hand-held tools of the widespread core tool and scraper tradition.[5] A few early sites like Upper Swan, Malanggangerr, and perhaps Seton on Kangaroo Island, have a simple stone flake technology; some flakes in the semi-arid areas show the first suggestions of desert specialisations by around 18,000 years ago in the form of adze flakes; some strange large tools exist at various places — edge-ground hatchets in the north but not in the south, the Kartan on open sites where pebbles and blocks of stone are available, in some cases dated to as late as 7000 years ago, and possibly associated with the megafauna. Bone points are found in Tasmania during the Pleistocene, but they disappear during the Holocene.

In all of these Pleistocene and early Holocene technological and economic specialisations, nowhere is there any evidence that megafauna were actively hunted, or that fire was being used to manage the landscape. Indeed, virtually all the Australian pollen cores show low charcoal levels right throughout the period when the megafauna become extinct. Not only do we lack hard evidence supporting Aboriginal hunting of megafauna, but we also lack hard evidence supporting the use of fire by Aborigines during the Pleistocene.

Defining the megafauna

There are three questions we must address before we can evaluate the impact of Aborigines on the megafauna — what were the megafauna, what is extinction as far as it applies to them, and when did this extinction take place? These questions are intimately linked, because it has been suggested that dwarfing of some megafaunal populations did occur, and that, for example, the presumed extinct *Macropus titan* and the extant *Macropus giganteus* are in fact one in the same species.[6]

Extinction of a species is the loss of that species from the living world. Tied up with this concept is the idea that species exist independently of one another, and that each species has evolved from an ancestral species. The factors which influence speciation, such as isolation of populations, divergence, selection pressure, founder population size, all need to be kept in mind during an evaluation of what is extinction, but in essence an animal becomes extinct if there are no longer any descendants which are taxonomically identifiable as belonging to the same species.

In the megafaunal extinction debate, it is not at all clear whether all of the Australian megafauna have left no descendants. For example, we know that many forms like koalas, goannas and echidnas had larger closely related or possibly identical species or ancestors living during the middle to late Pleistocene. The problem arises because we can see extant species, and test their genetic make-up, but we can't try to cross-breed them with extinct species to which they may be closely related in order to determine whether in fact they are two separate species or two size variants within a single breeding population.

The most obvious example of a mechanism by which a species can give rise to animals which are sufficiently morphologically different to be classified, rightly or wrongly, as a different species is the process of neoteny — the ability of juvenile forms of animals to breed, and the preferential survival of smaller animals. One consequence is that if breeding can occur in younger and therefore smaller animals, the new populations become dwarfed. In times of stress, particularly in the situations where water availability is low or where the larger animals are being selectively removed from the population — for example, by hunting — there is a selection pressure which favours neoteny and smaller individuals. This phenomenon is particularly common in island populations — for example, mammoths off Siberia and California and red deer on Jersey.[7] A question we must, therefore, ask ourselves is: did the reduction in standing water in Australia, which occurred with the increasing aridity during the terminal Pleistocene, create a series of land connected 'islands' of suitable habitat within Australia? If the grey kangaroo is a direct descendant of the *Macropus titan*, a megafaunal species, then either climate change or Aboriginal hunting pressure, or both, could have contributed to the selection of smaller animals.

The second question we must ask ourselves is: what are the megafauna? There are various definitions. Martin and Klein suggest that they were animals which approximated or exceeded 44 kg in weight, those animals which were under 44 kg are referred to as 'small'.[8] Others use 40 kg as the cut-off point, while others use loose definitions like the 'large extinct vertebrates of the Pleistocene'.[9]

Large animals became extinct right across the world at the end of the Pleistocene, and they did so in all continents, although the timing and the number of species which became extinct varied from place to place. Australia was no exception. In Australia, large forms of mammals, reptiles and birds all disappeared between 50,000 and 10,000 years ago, but it is in the mammals that the extinctions were greatest. Most of the animals which became extinct were large grazers or browsers, and most belonged to one of the two large herbivorous marsupial families — the Macropodidae and the Diprotidontidae. Although a number of smaller species of macropodids survived, the entire diprotodontid family succumbed to extinction. Among the genera which became extinct were *Diprotodon*, *Procoptodon*, *Nototherium*, *Palorchestes*, *Sthenurus* and *Protemnodon*.

Another extinct large form was *Thylacoleo*, a leopard-sized carnivore related to the possums. It is important to note that most workers exclude the *Thylacine* and *Sarcophilus*, the Tasmanian devil, from these arguments, since one is still extant and the other may still be extant, or at least it was until within the last 60 years. Their extinction on the mainland was a Holocene event which occurred much later (in the case of the *Sarcophilus*, less than 500 years ago), and was more likely related to the arrival of an important competitor for their particular carnivorous niches, the dingo.[10]

The megafauna were not uniformly distributed across the country. It is clear that they were concentrated in a broad band which excluded two habitat zones — the northern rainforests and the Central Australian arid zone. At least some species, including Diprotodontids, occurred in New Guinea. There may also be a gap between southeastern Australia and the populations which existed in western New South Wales and the eastern parts of South Australia. To what extent these distributions are biased by poor preservation of fossils, or indeed inadequate survey, is not clear. What is clear is that the megafauna were widespread during the Pleistocene until 40,000 years ago.

The extinction process did not occur everywhere at the same time. Many species which had been stable since the Tertiary period became extinct within the space of a few thousand years, but in some areas a few species seem to have survived much later. The animals in the driest zones, in places like Lake Callabonna in South Australia, appear to have become extinct by around 40,000 years ago. Those from places like Lake Mungo, where only *Procoptodon* remains have been found, and the Willandra Lakes system, seem to be gone by about 19,000 years ago. In the east, one species classed as megafauna survived at Clogg's Cave until 18,000 years ago; in the south, at Kangaroo Island, *Sthenurus*, the flat-faced kangaroo, survived until 16,000 years ago; but in the Liverpool Plains area of northern New South Wales a range of megafaunal species including *Diprotodon* seemed to have survived well into the Holocene, until around 6500 years ago, according to Richard Wright.[11]

In summary, the megafauna were a range of large species of vertebrates, including mammals, birds and reptiles, which were widespread across Australia. Extinction for them appears to have been a gradual process, with several species surviving in some areas until after 20,000 years ago, and possibly into the Holocene in northern New South Wales. There is a strong possibility that at least one existing species, the grey kangaroo, is a dwarfed form of a megafaunal species, *Macropus titan*, in which case there is at least one species of megafauna which avoided extinction by becoming smaller.

Having established the parameters of megafaunal extinction, there are three basic models of extinction which need to be evaluated — climate change, Aboriginal burning and Aboriginal overhunting. A fourth option is that some combination of these factors resulted in the extinctions.

Climate change

The first model of megafaunal extinctions in Australia to be considered suggests that the large animals could not adapt to the arid conditions at the end of the Pleistocene. Being large, it may be that they were dependent of large volumes of water, which needed to be available year-round. On this basis, megafauna may have been absent from parts of the tropical north because of the long dry season during the winter months, when no rain falls. Rainfall is more regular in the south but, as Wright has argued, the best place for year-round regular and abundant rainfall in Australia, at least during the Holocene, is the Liverpool Plains in northern New South Wales, which is exactly where the most recent megafauna seem to have survived.[12] It is also relevant that some of the best preserved megafaunal sites are associated with swamps and lakes.

It is clear that the extinctions did occur during times of climatic stress, both in general terms and, in a few cases, where specific or localised aridity has been shown to have occurred simultaneously with megafaunal extinctions — for example, Lancefield and Tambar

Springs.[13] But what is increasing aridity really doing? What was the range of environments existing in Australia at the end of the Pleistocene? Seasonality and unreliability of rainfall may well have been a problem in some areas, but surely there were large tracts of land which could still support at least some of the large megafauna species. It has to be assumed that there have always been swamps somewhere in Australia. The availability and necessity for water certainly appears to be a major factor in determining the distribution and population density of large species. Populations of the red kangaroo increased dramatically when Europeans introduced extra watering holes in the arid zone.[14]

Habitat destruction is another possibility. If the long-term aridity resulted in a contraction of the megafaunal populations into a few suitable environments, it is not difficult to imagine that those few areas of suitable habitat would have been eaten out fairly quickly, leaving the population to diminish because of starvation. After all, large animals need a great deal of food to support themselves, and if they are not particularly mobile, this could certainly become a major problem. Certainly large-scale population reductions would put species in a position where they were far more vulnerable to other factors such as disease or overhunting.

One of the indicators of environmental stress in animals is disease. It was reported that 7.5% of fossils at Lancefield showed some evidence of disease.[15] It is also important to note that the vast majority of the species which became extinct were grazing animals, suggesting that if loss of food resources was a major component, then there must have been extensive changes occurring in the vegetation. If it were possible for palynologists to identify what plants were present before and after the megafauna became extinct, then it may be possible to decide if climate-induced vegetation change was the major contributing factor. Some answers might come from the work presently being undertaken at Cuddie Springs in northern New South Wales, where human occupation, megafauna, stone tools with blood and hair residues, and pollen are all found preserved together at around 19,000 years ago.[16]

The strongest argument against climate change as being the sole cause of the extinctions is that these animals had survived such fluctuations before, throughout the 2 million years of the Pleistocene. Why did they finally die out this time?

An important ecological consideration in this debate is that the niches of large browsing herbivores remained unfilled until Europeans introduced cattle. Therefore competitive exclusion is not a factor which needs to be taken into account.

David Horton, a palaeoecologist, is a strong advocate of the climate-change model. He believes that the economy of the first Australians was not a coastal one, but a more general one which could adapt to exploit whatever resources were available, but particularly small game. His view is that the larger the game, the more difficult to catch, the less likely to be hunted. Horton suggests that, initially, the Aboriginal population of Australia was largely restricted to the well-watered woodlands which, until the increased aridity which took place between 30,000 and 25,000 years ago, meant about two-thirds of the continent (with the exception of the arid centre).[17]

Horton believes that the high productivity of the woodland areas, associated with the ready availability of water (water always within a day's walk), made the woodlands particularly attractive to hunter-gatherers. His model infers that at this time Aboriginal people did not use containers for transporting water, or did not exploit buried sources of water like wells, but were dependent on the daily availability of surface water, in exactly the same way that the megafauna were.

The second stage of his model relates to the time period between around 25,000 and 12,000 years ago. During this phase, the climate became much drier and windier, and the increased aridity would have restricted the Aboriginal population to the coastal fringes. He believes the same process contributed to the extinction of the megafauna. Climate is seen to be the primary cause of the megafaunal extinctions.

The third phase of Horton's model sees the human population spreading throughout the continent as the climate becomes milder, and he suggests that the development or introduction of new technology may well have contributed to the successful use of what were previously marginal or inhospitable areas. By implication, by the time Aborigines recolonised these marginal areas the megafauna were already extinct.

An interesting analogy exists between Horton's model and Bowlder's model of coastal colonisation.[18] Both suggest that, between 25,000 and 12,000 years ago, human occupation of Australia should be restricted to the coastal strip. The inference here is that most Australian prehistorians and archaeologists believe that there were marked changes in the distribution of all the Australian fauna, as well as the human population. Presumably there was a corresponding difficulty in obtaining food for humans and megafauna, but they were not competing with each other directly, although the model invoking Aboriginal burning as a cause for megafaunal extinction implies that Aboriginal burning may have modified the vegetation so that the megafauna had no food — in which case the extinction events would be an example of indirect competition.

In order to explain the distribution of human habitation sites in Central Australia during the Pleistocene, Peter Veth suggests that the desert culture which existed in the arid zone was in fact a very dynamic one and is associated with changes in land use, demography and technology.[19] Veth argues that the arid zone should be viewed in terms of refuges, barriers and corridors. Refuges are areas which provide reliable sources of water; barriers are the large sandridge deserts with uncoordinated drainage; and corridors are seen as those areas of stony and sandy desert which would have been occupied during the less extreme climatic conditions, but abandoned during the glacial maximum.[20] If we superimpose the megafauna on this model, and assume that megafauna had an even greater need for reliable sources of water, their refuges may have been in the coastal margins and the better watered areas in northern New South Wales.

The most recent megafauna remains seem to come from the Gunnedah area of New South Wales near Lime Springs and Trinkey, where *Diprotodon* remains have been dated to 7000 years ago.[21] Richard Wright suggests that the reason the megafauna survived in this area is that there is good year-round rainfall in this region, a situation which does not occur further north (with high summer and low winter rainfall) or further south (with high winter and low summer).

This association between the availability of regular water and late survival of the megafauna has been made by several researchers who think that the increasing aridity, coupled with the modifications in vegetation induced by Aboriginal burning and Aboriginal hunting, ultimately led to their extinction — a combination of factors which had never before presented itself in Australia. Since the late Pleistocene changes were of greater magnitude than earlier ones, they resulted in the extinctions which had not previously occurred, although presumably the megafaunal would have gone through a number of cycles during the Pleistocene where their population and distributions first increased, then decreased.

Taken in isolation, there is apparently no need to invoke any cause other than climate change to be able to explain the extinctions. Even if Aborigines were not part of the Australian environment, it is reasonable to assume that increasing aridity would result in a decrease in the water supply, a decrease in the standing crop of vegetation, and a decrease in the biomass of herbivores which could be supported by that lower amount of vegetation. In the extreme climatic conditions at around 18,000 years ago, it is possible, indeed likely, that at least some of the megafauna would become extinct.

If, as Horton and others suggest, the megafauna were basically woodland and open-forest animals, then clearly there are several places where we would not expect to find them by 18,000 years ago — certainly not in the arid interior.[22] But where would we expect to find them? Surely predominantly along the better watered east coast. And what do we find in this area today? Some of it is under the Pacific Ocean. It is probable that the megafauna survived longest in the woodlands and open-forest remnants which remained between the coast and the Great Dividing Range. The other critical point is that there are few sites along the east coast where megafaunal remains are likely to be preserved. They are found in high pH soils, particularly limestones regions and alkaline lacustrine deposits, and there are few of these along the east coast.

The other environment where megafauna are likely to be preserved is in swamps and bogs, and these are also few. Interestingly, one of the areas where swamps and bogs are common is the Liverpool Plains area, where at least four sites show relatively late megafauna — Trinkey, Lime Springs, Cuddie Springs, and Tambar Springs. Crucial to this argument is the seasonality and regularity of rainfall. Long periods of drought can indeed cause the extinction, at least locally, of many species. Indeed, those large animals which survive in the semi-arid zone today, the red kangaroo and the emu, have evolved physiological mechanisms to cope with periods of drought.[23]

If these are the arguments in favour of a climate-induced extinction, what are the arguments against it? First, it is not at all clear why at least some of the megafauna could not have survived in refuges within the well-watered eastern coastal plain — or indeed, as Wright argues, in the Liverpool Plains area — until the Holocene. If conditions were becoming gradually wetter after 18,000 years ago, and we know that at least some of the megafauna survived at places like Kangaroo Island until 16,000 years ago, what was to prevent them from recolonising the newly available habitats again? Crucial to this argument is which species survived in which areas. Leaving aside the northern New South Wales sites, and if we accept that *Macropus titan* is indeed the direct ancestor of *Macropus giganteus*, what are we left with in the remainder of the continent?

There do not appear to be examples of the megafauna younger than around 30,000 in Western Australia.[24] There are diprotodons at Spring Creek in Victoria and on Kangaroo Island at 19,000, but not later.[25] *Sthenurus* (the flat faced kangaroo), *Protemnodon* and *Zygomaturus*, were present in Tasmania and on Kangaroo Island 19,000 years ago.[26] *Sthenurus* was still present on Kangaroo Island 16,000 years ago.[27]

At another megafauna site, Cuddie Springs, the fauna includes *Diprotodon*, *Sthenurus*, *Protemnodon* and a giant goanna, but detailed publication is needed before the exact dates of the megafauna are known. It certainly appears that some are as late as 19,000 years ago.[28]

In summary, other than Wright's site, there are no clear diprotodontids or their close relatives after around 19,000 years ago, and the only other large animal which does survive after this period appears to be the *Sthenurus*, which were not all that much bigger than the extant grey and red kangaroos. The critical time therefore appears to be around 18,000, exactly when aridity was at its worst. A few of the larger kangaroos managed to survive a little longer, but that is all.

What are we to make of the 6500 year-old date for *Diprotodon* at Tambar Springs. There are two things to note. First, the remains are all tooth enamel, not bone; and secondly, their demise corresponds to an arid phase at the lake. There is always a possibility that either the diprotodontid teeth enamel has been reworked or the radiocarbon dates are incorrect. A small amount of recent contamination can make old carbon look much younger than it is. If the arid phase of the lake is 18,000 years old, not 6500 years old and for which there is no equivalent severe arid period recorded elsewhere in Australia, then these data may fit the pattern. In any event, it seems that the case for climate as being the causative agent for the megafaunal extinctions is stronger, not weaker, when we assess the evidence without considering the possibility of human intervention.

Fire

Both Gurdip Singh and Peter Kershaw believe they can detect the initiation of Aboriginal burning on the basis of massively increased charcoal in their pollen cores, Singh suggesting that the Lake George area was first burnt more than 120,000 years ago, and Kershaw believing that he has detected the arrival of Aborigines on the Atherton Tableland in North Queensland around 38,000 years ago.[29] They base their evidence on an increase in the amount of charcoal. Yet other workers, like Robyn Clark, believe they can detect the abandonment of some areas on the basis of an increase in charcoal in pollen cores.[30] The problem we face is that the interpretation of pollen cores is highly subjective, and the opposite conclusions can be drawn from essentially the same data. How then is it possible to suggest that Aboriginal burning, for which there is no direct evidence and equivocal indirect evidence, was a major factor in the extinction process?

Rhys Jones argues that Aborigines, with their firestick farming, modified the landscape and that this, in addition to overhunting, led to the demise of the megafauna.[31] Clark believes that the impact of Aborigines on the environment, at least during the Pleistocene, was minimal and almost insignificant when compared to the changes which were induced by climate.[32] It is also obvious that the megafauna would have been exposed to fire before Aborigines arrived in Australia. Fire has been a component of the Australian biota for a considerable period of time. Much of the Australian vegetation is fire-adapted, or at least fire-resistant. It is inconceivable that any increase in fire frequency could modify the vegetation to the extent that virtually all the large animals became extinct in all environments. After all, megafauna existed right across the country at various times in all the watered woodlands, including some cool areas like Tasmania and the Southern Highlands.

The model which is favoured by Kershaw is that Aboriginal burning resulted in megafaunal habitat destruction. Even if we accept that Aboriginal burning was an important component of the late Pleistocene environment, it simply reinforced the trends initiated by climate change. Aborigines did not burn contrary to the direction in which the climate was pushing the vegetation. The result of both increasing aridity and increased Aboriginal burning would be an increase in savannah-grasslands, and these areas were highly productive for large browsers — for example, antelope and elephants in Africa. But what did the megafauna eat? If they were grazers, firestick farming may have improved their environment. Why would burning cause only the extinction of the larger game? Why not small game as well? Kershaw argues that changes to the plant communities induced by fire may have contributed to the demise of the megafauna, but if animals like diprodotons were grazing in swamps, would Aboriginal burning have had any impact? Flannery argues that once the megafauna became extinct, the vegetation changed in response to the removal of the large herbivores.[33] Clearly there is no easy answer to this complex set of issues.

Even if we accept the hypothesis that Aboriginal burning did impact on the vegetation and that this began, say, 38,000 years ago, as has been suggested for Lynch's Crater, then the megafauna survived for at least another 20,000 years after the start of Aboriginal burning. If Singh is correct, they survived for 100,000 years after Aboriginal burning began. Clearly, even if we accept the hypothesis that Aboriginal burning modified the landscape, there is little to support the view that this in turn directly caused the extinction of the megafauna. The period of coexistence is just too long.

White and O'Connell sum up the argument with the following: 'While it [Aboriginal burning] may have interfered with breeding or lifestyles in some areas, it seems unlikely to have been the sole cause of extinction throughout Sahul.'[34]

Pleistocene overkill

A third model supports the contention that Aboriginal hunting directly caused the extinction of the megafauna. First we need to consider whether Aborigines could successfully exploit the terrestrial environment without hunting the megafauna. Horton certainly believes they could — in the woodlands. Bowdler certainly believes they could — along the coasts. Did they have the capacity to exploit the megafauna, or indeed did they have the inclination or was it necessary to do so? What were the practical limitations regarding the hunting of the megafauna? If they were hunted, did they not retreat from man? Why do we not find examples of kill sites or butchery sites? Indeed, where would we expect to find them? Perhaps in the woodlands, where David Horton's model suggests they would be found?

There are many known archaeological sites with megafaunal remains associated with them (see Table 1). Certainly at Mammoth Cave in Western Australia there are burnt bones and cut marks suggesting that Aborigines were eating at least some megafauna 37,000 years ago, but this does not necessarily mean that they were hunting megafaunal species.[35]

Table 1

Sites where megafauna and humans may have co-existed

Site	Megafaunal taxa	Date (approx)
Keilor	Most megafauna	>36,000
Lake Tandou	Most megafauna extinct	27,000
Lancefield	Most megafauna	26,000
Lake Menindee	Most megafauna	25–16,000
Cloggs Cave	Sthenurus	23,000
Beginners Luck	Macropus titan	20,600
Lime Springs	Diprotodon, Procoptodon, Stenthurus, Macropus titan, Protemnodon.	<19,300
Rocky River	Stenthurus, Diprotodon, Protemnodon, Zygomaturus	19,000
Cuddie Springs	Stenthurus, Diprotodon, Protemnodon	19,000
Seton	Stenthurus	16,000
Trinkey	Diprotodon	7,000

It must be assumed that killing and butchering of megafauna would take place in the open. Evidence for hunting might therefore be found in the open, particularly near swamps where large animals would tend to congregate.

One factor which needs to be considered is the reproductive rate of the megafauna. If this was low, as it the case with many large animals, then in a situation where there are no predators, a low reproductive rate is of no concern. However, if a predator begins to harvest these animals, the low reproductive rate, coupled with the decrease in the population, can lead to a rapid reduction in the large-animal population. Saul reported on computer models which suggested that mammoths and humans coexisted in North America until the human population increased to a certain level, after which the mammoth population fell dramatically to extinction.[36] Low levels of hunting may be all that is needed to reduce prey populations. Saul estimated that an annual harvesting rate of 3–4% for mammoths would maintain the population, but harvesting rates in excess of that figure would cause the population to decline. Winter carried out a similar calculation and showed that harvesting rates above 15% per annum would cause a decline in kangaroo populations.[37]

It has also been suggested that the megafauna were easy to hunt because they had not been exposed to human predators. This naivety would make them vulnerable to overhunting. The difficulty here is: how long would it take them to learn that Aborigines intended to harm them? Aborigines could not cause the extinction of the water buffalo in the Northern Territory once they were introduced in the 1820s, nor did they cause the extinction of the feral cattle which escaped in the Sydney region in 1788.[38] If Aborigines with highly developed technologies could not cause the extinction of these large herbivorous mammals, starting from a small population base, it seems unlikely that they could have caused the extinction of the megafauna, all other factors being equal.

An extreme position is taken by Martin and Flannery, who support the view that 'Pleistocene overkill' was caused by Aborigines hunting and killing the megafauna to extinction.[39] One crucial part of their argument is that the megafauna were quickly wiped out by Aboriginal hunting. It is difficult to support this suggestion, since evidence has steadily accumulated that at many places in many different environments, the megafauna coexisted with man for perhaps as long as 40,000 years. There was not a rapid and widespread extinction — rather there were localised extinctions in some environments, while in other areas the megafauna appeared to flourish or at least to be supporting viable populations. The late finds, in many cases associated with Aboriginal cultural remains, put a rather large hole in Martin's argument for rapid extinction. If the Aborigines caused the megafauna to become extinct, they did it over a period of perhaps at least 20,000 and perhaps 30–40,000 years.

Trophic cascade

In 1990, Flannery published a paper which acted as a focus for many of the divergent ideas which had been floating around in the literature, but which had never really been synthesised, with the exception of David Horton's review some ten years earlier.[40] Flannery argued that Aborigines had indeed rapidly hunted the megafauna to extinction; that subsequently the removal of the large herbivores resulted in changes in the vegetation; and that Aboriginal burning was introduced in order to compensate for the changes in the vegetation.

Flannery is a supporter of Martin's 'blitzkrieg' hypothesis, and believes that all of the megafauna were killed within a few thousand years of Aborigines arriving in Australia. He argues that with the rapid extinction of the megafauna, virtually all of which were herbivorous, a great deal of vegetation was left uneaten, increasing the standing crop of fuel. As a consequence, fires became larger and hotter than before, causing the reduction on fire-sensitive plants to the advantage of those which were fire-resistant or indeed fire-dependant.

Flannery suggests that Aborigines then began to burn more frequently, firestick farming if you like, in order to maintain a high species diversity and to reduce the impact of high intensity fires on medium-sized animals and perhaps some plants. He argues that twentieth-century Australian mammal extinctions are largely the result of the cessation of firestick farming.

His model has a number of problems. He has to accept that Aboriginal burning started virtually at the same time everywhere, if indeed the megafauna were rapidly extinguished shortly after Aborigines arrived. He must then accept the evidence of the palynologists. In comparing Singh's Lake George data with Kershaw's Lynch's Crater data, Flannery says: 'Although there are difficulties with precise temporal correlations between the two localities, they both show the same pattern of change.' Indeed they do, but this difficulty with precise temporal correlations is in the order of 80,000 years! — 120,000 years ago for Lake George and 38,000 years ago for Lynch's Crater. To muddy the waters further, one of the sites which describes megafaunal remains in Victoria 19,000 years ago, Spring Creek, was published by Beth Gott, a palynologist, and Tim Flannery.[41] In 1984 Flannery claimed that megafauna existed in Victoria 19,000 years ago, yet in 1990 he argued that all the megafauna were extinct by around 35,000 years ago. It is difficult to reconcile these two accounts, although recent investigations at the Spring Creek site indicate that there may be problems associated with the dating of the deposits and the fossils which they contain.[42]

What killed the megafauna?

There are three conflicting models of megafaunal extinction. Flannery believes in the overkill hypothesis, Kershaw attempts to explain the nature of the Australian vegetation as well as megafaunal extinctions based on hypothetical Aboriginal burning, and Horton relies on climate. In summary:

1. Climate worsened, reaching the most inhospitable and driest at the height of the glacial period around 18,000 years ago.

2. Fire became more common as the climate deteriorated, resulting in vegetation associations which were more susceptible to fire.

3. Many large animals became extinct, most between 30,000 and 18,000 years ago.

4. A few megafaunal species, notably some large macropods, survived until at least 16,000 years ago, and possibly into the Holocene on the Liverpool Plains in northern New South Wales.

5. It is possible that some *Macropus titan* may have dwarfed into *Macropus giganteus*, an extant species.

6. Some species of large macropods, particularly the red kangaroo and the euro, did survive until the present, as did the emu. (If they had become extinct, we would have called them megafauna).

7. There is no direct evidence that Aborigines actively hunted the megafauna during the Pleistocene.

8. There is some evidence that Aborigines may have butchered and eaten megafauna around the margins of swamps.

9. Refuge areas probably existed to which megafauna could retreat.

10. Both Aboriginal and megafauna species probably retreated to the better watered areas at the height of the arid period.

The strongest evidence seems to support the model that climate change was the dominant factor in causing the megafauna to become extinct. Aboriginal use of fire may have had some marginal effect, but it probably had no effect at all. Once the megafaunal populations were reduced, and the Aboriginal population had also contracted, the exploitation of megafauna as a food source may well have increased, but the evidence is not yet clear whether they were actively hunted, killed when they became trapped in swamps, or scavenged after they died. In any event, it appears that the additional pressure of an Aboriginal presence in Australia may have tipped the scale in favour of extinction rather than recovery after the last glacial maximum, where previously the populations had recovered.

The last refuge for the megafauna was in the south (Victoria, Tasmania and Kangaroo Island), where there was a high rainfall level all year round, and in the Liverpool Plains area of New South Wales, where there was a regular rainfall in both the summer and winter months. The earliest extinctions, which may have occurred before 40,000 years ago, took place in the semi-arid zone, and once the lakes dried out the megafauna disappeared. If Wright's interpretation is correct, the last great drying event took seems to have taken place during the Holocene around 6500 years ago, and this marked the final demise of the remnants of the large fauna.

As the temperatures warmed, the sea levels rose, the rainfall increased and a new Holocene vegetation association became firmly established. The increase in Aboriginal burning which seems to be detectable from this time was probably associated with the introduction or invention of new technologies which allowed Aboriginal people to concentrate on those large resources which were previously so difficult to capture — kangaroos and large wallabies.

Fire was initially used to promote and retain the environments which were most suitable for these animals, and fire was subsequently used for maximising the productivity of these areas after the massive Aboriginal population increase which occurred largely because of the greater access to this abundant resource.

There is considerable doubt as to whether Aboriginal people played any part in the extinction of the megafauna, or indeed whether or not they created any significant environmental impacts during the Pleistocene. It is not until the Holocene, when temperatures warmed, sea levels stabilised, rainfall increased, populations increased and technological change occurred, that there is evidence for significant Aboriginal environmental impact.

CHAPTER 6

Technological change and Aboriginal economy

Hunting and gathering have formed the basis of the economic system which humans have been using for most of the last several hundred thousand years. A second economic system, based on agriculture and herding, is dependent on the domestication of animal and plants, and the environmental consequences of this economic system can be much greater. The processes associated with growing crops and herding animals began less then 10,000 years ago, but it is sometimes difficult to distinguish between the two systems. In Australia, Aboriginal people have always used hunting and gathering as their basic mode of subsistence.

Hunting

The human species has always been a hunter. For at least the last 500,000 years there is clear archaeological evidence that human populations hunted a diverse range of animals.[1] Up until around 10,000 years ago, all human populations across the world depended primarily on hunting for their main sources of protein. Meat has been an important part of the human diet for at least 2 million years. Many essential vitamins and minerals are obtained from animal foods, and there is little doubt that many of the physiological adaptations which have evolved in the human digestive system are directed towards consuming both plant and animal foods.

It was the use of some types of stone tools which enabled man to become an efficient hunter. He could use the tools directly to be thrown at other animals. He could use the sharp stone flakes to cut up the meat, and he could also use the flakes to sharpen wooden spear tips and to shape clubs. In the latter stages of human development the sharp flakes were used as spear points and barbs.

Using wood, bone, shell, animal hides and stone, an enormous array of tools was developed to hunt game. Clubs, spears, harpoons, bows and arrows, blowpipes, nets and traps have been developed in different parts of the world to hunt a variety of game, from small lizards and fish to elephants and whales. Indeed, almost every animal species has been actively hunted by someone, sometime, somewhere. In a few societies, anything which was edible and which was found close by was included in the diet, but in other human populations the range of animals selected for hunting was smaller.

In some cases, an additional technological process was invoked to make hunting more efficient. Particularly in parts of South America, southeast Asia, Africa and in Australia, poisons were used to assist with hunting. Some of the poisons were so lethal that even small amounts could kill large animals. With the assistance of poisons and a bow and arrow, a Bushman hunter could kill an elephant.

If hunting is such an important component of human survival strategies, then there must be valid reasons why it has continued to play such an important role in most human societies. Any food is of value only if it provides calories — that is, it contains organic materials which can be converted into energy. The three principal forms of energy storage in biological organisms are proteins, fats and carbohydrates. As with all other living organisms, humans require energy to carry out basic bodily functions — muscular activity, growth, maintaining body temperature. If the energy to carry out these processes is not provided by the intake of food, then fat reserves within the body are consumed. If the fat reserves are depleted, as is the case in acute malnutrition, the protein which makes up the body's tissues is itself consumed.

Hunting is therefore one way of providing the body with a source of energy, and any excess energy which is created can be stored by the body as fat, for later use. Fat is a far more effective storage mechanism because it is not bound up with water the way carbohydrates and proteins are. On a gram for gram basis, it is six times as efficient at storing energy.

Plants can provide carbohydrates in large quantities, and cereals, fruits and starchy roots have probably been components of the human diet for longer than meat. They can also provide some protein, particularly in the form of nuts. But essentially, protein and fat are generally acquired in the human diet through animal food. The major human dietary sources of protein are meat, fish and eggs, and hunting is required for the first two of these. Eggs will generally only be seasonally available under natural conditions, so hunting and fishing are most important mechanisms by which proteins and fats are acquired.

For animal foods, in terms of the amount of energy contained in equivalent amounts of tissue, fat is the most efficient, because it contains on average 9.3 kilocalories (kcal) per gram, whereas proteins and carbohydrates contain about 4 kcal per gram.[2] However, there are eight essential amino acids which humans cannot synthesise, and these must be taken into the body in the form of protein, almost all of which is derived from animal tissue.

It would seem that the most biologically appropriate diet for humans is one where there is a balance between plant foods and animal protein, but the animal protein does not necessarily have to come in the form of meat. It can come in the form of shellfish, eggs or insects, for example the witchetty grub which is eaten by many Aboriginal people.

So if it is not necessary to eat meat to satisfy the dietary requirements in terms of essential amino acids, vitamins and minerals, why have humans spent so much time hunting? Perhaps the answer lies in the fact that a large animal contains enough energy to supply a large number of people for several days. In terms of the amount of energy expended and the amount of energy obtained, hunting can be very rewarding. However, there is a trade-off. What if you go hunting and you don't catch anything? This can be disastrous if you are relying on your hunting ability to survive. While you may be able to survive without food for a few days, it does not take long for the lack of food to produce weakness, which in turn limits the capacity to hunt.

Humans have evolved different strategies for overcoming this problem, and we find at least four of them in traditional Aboriginal society — cooperative hunting, to maximise the chance of success; community sharing of those animals which have been caught; hunting a wide range of different prey species; and a division of labour so that while the men are out hunting, the women and children gather plant foods, insects and small game to ensure that there would always be something to eat. The other option for ensuring a regular supply of food, which Aboriginal people did not adopt, is domestication of animals and farming.

Hunting clearly has some impacts on the environment. There are several factors which need to be considered. The extent of the impact will depend on the technology used to exploit the prey, the size of the human population relative to the size of the prey population, and the sensitivity of the prey population to reduction in numbers through hunting. These are complex issues, because we need to consider not only the predator and prey population densities, but ecological variability within any particular area.

Some hunting technologies can have catastrophic effects on the prey population. One technique for hunting bison which was employed by native Americans was to drive the entire herd over a cliff and then butcher the best cuts of meat from the animals at the top of the pile, leaving the remainder of the herd to decompose.[3] Such a technology certainly had an impact on the herd that was hunted, because it ceased to exist, but, like all predator–prey relationships, this type of catastrophic hunting technique could only be used while the bison herds were present. It may have taken 50 years to replace the number of animals which were killed, although the population of bison was probably able to recover from such catastrophes by migration from surrounding areas. A similar technique was reported for Aboriginal people in the lower Blue Mountains west of Sydney, who drove wallabies along a ridge and over a cliff into the Nepean River Gorge.[4]

The bison hunting is a rare example where only a small proportion of the animals killed in a hunt were consumed. In general, whatever was killed was eaten. Under these circumstances, the important factor was the ratio of hunters to prey. The larger the number of hunters, the greater likelihood of a particular animal being killed. The larger the number of hunters, the more likely that the prey population would be threatened.

The proportion of animals in the prey population which could be culled annually without impacting on the survival of the population varies from species to species, depending on such things as reproductive rates, age structure and sex ratio of the community. For a population of 100 grey kangaroos, all things being equal, in the absence of hunting the population will increase by about fifteen individuals per year. This means that a stable population would be one where no more than fifteen individuals were culled annually. However, if the fifteen animals killed were all reproductive females, this rate of harvesting would cause a decline in the population. If the animals were all immature males, the loss would have little impact, at least in the short term.[5]

Provided that the population of hunters was low, and the population of prey was moderately large, then a hunting strategy which removed the occasional animal from the population would have no serious long-term effects. However, strategies which involve either total destruction or overexploitation of a prey population, or the modification of the environment which supports that population, may well have consequences beyond the short term effects resulting from direct hunting. Such strategies may be particularly important in three situations — where there are small geographically isolated prey populations, such as on islands; where the prey populations are adapted to a narrow range of microhabitats; and where the prey population has not previously come in contact with predators.

Gathering

In hunter-gatherer societies, women generally collect the smaller but more readily available resources which provide the dietary staples, in order to provide an adequate supply of food even if the men have been successful in their hunting. The actual foods gathered almost certainly depended on what resources were locally abundant, and a seasonal pattern of land use applied in most temperate and arid areas.

As is the case with contemporary hunter-gatherer communities in Australia and elsewhere, there is of necessity a seasonal mobility inherent in a successful hunter-gatherer economy. Some resources will be seasonally abundant at one area, and others will be plentiful somewhere else at a different time of the year. Seasonal occupation of selected areas by hunter-gatherers was recognised by Charles Darwin, who observed the Tierra del Fuegans at the southern tip of South America. Darwin states: 'The inhabitants, living chiefly upon shell-fish, are obliged constantly to change their place of residence, but they return at intervals to the same spot, as is evident from the piles of old shells, which must often amount to many tons of weight.'[6]

As is common with hunter–gatherers around the world who live near the coast (with the possible exception of parts of Western Australia), shellfish provided an abundant and easily gathered source of protein. From the ethnographic data available on recent and contemporary Aboriginal exploitation of shellfish, we know that women predominantly gathered shellfish while the men fished or hunted marine or terrestrial animals.[7]

Probably the best study which has been carried out on Aboriginal people's gathering strategies was undertaken by Betty Meehan, who lived with the Gidjingali people of Arnhem Land from July 1972 to July 1973. She found that the occupation of sites could be divided into two types — 'home bases' and 'dinner-time' camps. Dinner-time camps 'are small camp sites used during middle of the day while people are engaged in hunting trips away from their home base. At these sites they cook and eat food that has been procured up until that time.'[8] Many of these camps were locations where shellfish were eaten, and when the sites were revisited regularly they accumulated discarded shells in the form of shell middens. Some 29 different species of shell fish were collected by the Gidjingali women.

The month of October had the lowest number of shellfish-gathering trips, but the weight of shellfish was the highest. No significant differences occurred in the amount collected in the wet season and the dry season, but shellfish were more important during the wet season because less of other types of food was available.

In the twelve months that Meehan carried out her study, the group, which averaged around 35 people, collected more than 6.7 tonnes of shellfish. The average calorific contribution from shellfish was slightly more than 1000 kcal per day, or 1800 kcal on those days when shellfish were gathered. Put another way, when women collected the bivalve Tapes, the tapestry shell, each woman collected on average 11.5 kg gross weight per day, equivalent to 2.4 kg of flesh, or 0.5 kg of protein, or 1920 kcal. A woman could provide enough energy for herself for a day by gathering this shellfish for two hours. Overall, for the entire population and for the entire year, shellfish contributed 14% of the daily energy allowance.[9]

In terms of the importance of vegetable food in the diet, Meehan's study suggests that vegetable foods contributed 57% of the energy to the Anbarra people she worked with, and animal foods made up 43%. For Central Australian communities, Meggitt estimated that vegetable foods were much more important, constituting 70–80% of the gross weight of food eaten.[10] Clearly, even within Australia there is enormous variation in the proportions of different plant and animal food which were eaten at different times and at different places.

Meehan recorded that no mammal meat was eaten at all during the month of May, which was referred to as 'fish time' by the Anbarra. The food consisted of plants, shellfish, shark, stingray, bony fish, goanna, pythons, turtle eggs and birds.

In terms of the mean daily caloric intake, Meehan based her study on an average figure of 2050 kcal being the recommended intake for these Aboriginal people. In the four months throughout the year in which she carried out detailed analysis, in only one month, January, was the caloric intake lower than the recommended, and even then she commented that no one seemed to be particularly hungry. During May, the intake was 122% of the recommended value.

The advantage of shellfish is that they are a reliable source of food, more so than fish or small game. Meehan suggests that wallabies and other land animals 'may be available only every four or five days at the most.'[11] Clearly shellfish gathering provides an important alternative to hunting large game and it therefore can be seen as a simple way of feeding a substantial number of people, providing that the shellfish are not being overexploited.

Meehan makes the following relevant observation:

> The actual time devoted to the gathering of shellfish on any one day is only about two hours... During that short time a skilled woman can collect shellfish equivalent to about 2000 kcal. For the rest of the day the women are free to participate in other activities if they so desire... Much of the time is spent in other foraging pursuits or in relaxing in the dinner-time camp.[12]

One interesting factor to emerge from her work with the Anbarra clan of the Gidjingali was that in 1973/74, the shellfish beds were destroyed by the fierce wet season and monsoons. Fresh water swept down the estuaries, totally annihilating all of the shellfish. As a consequence, the people collected more plant foods, wallabies, freshwater tortoises and goannas. These new combinations of foods 'provided a satisfactory diet'.[13]

In this situation, a 'natural' disaster certainly had a far greater impact than any Aboriginal gathering activity would have had, since the beds had been exploited annually and regularly for at least several decades prior to Meehan's research.

The other important factor relating to gathering is that there were social prohibitions against collective juvenile shellfish. These were referred to as 'babies', and when children collected them they were instructed to put them back in the shell beds. In this case, a social prohibition seems to have ensured that undersized specimens were not collected. This could well be viewed as a conservation mechanism. A similar prohibition regarding fruit occurs in both eastern Australia and Central Australia, where fruits which fall to the ground are not picked up by adults but left where they fall. They are referred to as 'dog food', because only dogs and little children are allowed to eat them.

Another possible conservation mechanism involved the gathering of yams. Aboriginal women would break off part of a yam and rebury it, so it would grow again the following year.[14]

Coupled with totemic prohibitions, which also restricted the number of animals which were hunted, at least for Aboriginal hunter-gatherers of the last few centuries, there seems to have been a series of cultural mechanisms in place to conserve specific resources. An extension of these prohibitions is to actually invest time and energy in looking after the resources, and this is exactly what herders and farmers began to do in other parts of the world, beginning around 10,000 years ago.

Aboriginal stone tool industries

For the most part, evidence of prehistoric Aboriginal activities is found in the form of stone tools. For a great part of the last 100 years, Australian prehistorians have been clinging to the ideas which were based on sequences of stone tools in Europe and the Middle East — the Eurocentric view of the world. Stone technologies were seen to follow a pattern, with the earliest stone tools being simple pebble choppers which evolved into handaxes and the addition of simple flake tools. These evolved into the more sophisticated flake tools, some with core preparation. Then there were the microlithic industries, followed by the last of the stone industries, which was characterised by finely manufactured knives and flint axes. These stone artefacts eventually gave rise to the bronze- and later iron-based technology.

When archaeologists found stone tools very similar to European types in Australia, it was natural for them to make comparisons. Small-backed blades and adze flakes were comparable to the Mesolithic, while edge-grinding was characteristic of the Neolithic. It came as quite a surprise when edge-ground axes were excavated in northern Australia dated to 22,000 years ago, 15,000 years before they were first used in Europe.[15]

There was a general recognition that perhaps Australian stone industries did not exactly fit the European pattern, and indeed during the 1950s and 1960s it became increasingly apparent that much of southeast Asia was very different from the rest of the world. By the mid-1970s it seemed clear that Australian stone-tool industries could be divided broadly into two stages — an early stage dominated by core tools and scrapers, and a later stage which included microlithic points and scrapers as well as backed blades. It was also recognised that there were some major changes taking place over the last 2000 years and that a variety of local stone and bone technologies had evolved. However, there was a general recognition of two divisions — big tools early and small tools later.

These two divisions were so distinctive and so widespread that they became known as the Australian core tool and scraper tradition for the earlier industry, and the Australian small tool tradition for the later industry.[16] The core tool and scraper tradition was based on the industry first described at Lake Mungo, and was characterised by horsehoof cores, steep scrapers made out of cores, steep scrapers made on flakes, sharp scrapers and large primary flakes.[17] The horsehoof cores and pebble tools, which were found where pebbles and gravels occurred, were presumed to have functioned as choppers for heavy woodworking.

The range of site types where the core tool and scraper assemblage was found was considerable, and it was identified in both rock shelters and open sites, in the arid zone, in woodlands, in forests, near coastal sites, in mountains and on the coastal plains. Some prehistorians make no distinction between these mainland industries and the stone industries found in Tasmania, which also contain crude choppers and scrapers.[18]

These tools were apparently hand-held rather than being hafted onto a handle, and it is surmised that they were primarily woodworking tools. They were therefore 'maintenance' tools — used in the process of manufacturing and maintaining other tools which were used directly to extract a living from the environment — the 'extractive' tools.

Around 4000 years ago, perhaps a little earlier in the north and a little later in the southeast, a whole new range of tool types, stoneworking techniques and cultural changes can be detected in the archaeological record. There is a massive increase in the amount of stone being used; a dramatic increase in the amount of waste for each tool produced; a dramatic decrease in the average size and weight of the waste flakes; and large numbers of sites used for the first time.[19] Rather than a uniformity across the continent, there are marked regional variations in the new tools, none of which ever reached Tasmania, which was already isolated from the mainland.

In Northern Australia, the Kimberley region and east as far as Arnhem Land, the new stone industry was characterised by the production of bifacially flaked points, some of which continued to be used into the ethnographic present. Further south, uniface points, known as pirri points, were widespread in South Australia and Victoria and across the arid zone into western New South Wales and southwestern Queensland. In the same region small geometric microliths were also found, and these were also used along the southeast coast, where they formed a component of an industry known as the Bondaian, named after Bondi Beach where the small-backed stone points called Bondi points were first recognised. At many sites in the southeast, elouera adze flakes were also found. Edge-ground axes are found in these sites associated with the small tool industries, but not before.[20]

The height of the microliths appears to have been between around 3500 and 1500 years ago. In many areas, particularly along the coast, they were no longer in use by 1500 years ago, although they were retained later in some places. During the last 1000–500 years, several forms disappeared altogether. Along the coastal strip of New South Wales, stone ceased to be used almost entirely and many of the functions of stone were replaced by shell or bone. Bone points became much more common, and on the basis of ethnography we know that these were used to barb multipronged fishing spears.[21]

In many regions the edge-ground hatchet became the dominant tool, while woodworking was carried out with hafted adze flakes, including the elouera along the east coast and certainly tula adze flakes across Central Australia. By the time Europeans arrived, diagnostic tools like Bondi points, pirri points and geometric microliths had all ceased to be manufactured and used.

The Kartan

The Kartan industry was first recognised in the 1920s. It was originally thought to be restricted to parts of Kangaroo Island (Karta) and the adjacent coast of South Australia, but examples have been found in the Flinders Ranges and possibly in northeastern New South Wales.[22] It was first recognised by Norman Tindale, who was then associated with the South Australian Museum.[23] It is characterised by the presence of large numbers of hammerstones and massive trimmed pebble implements. The average weight of a Kartan tool is around 900 grams, perhaps ten times the average of any other assemblage. By the end of the 1930s, 47 open camp sites containing the Kartan had been found on Kangaroo Island, and following more recent surveys there are over 120 known sites. The numbers of tools found at some sites was enormous, and one collector named Cooper collected 1400 pebble choppers and 150 hammerstones.[24]

The dominant tools of the Kartan are hammerstones and pebble choppers, but large heavy horsehoof cores, which in a smaller form occur as components of the core tool and scraper tradition, are also common. On Kangaroo Island, most of the Kartan tools are made of quartzite, which in many cases has been carried to the sites from up to 35 kilometres away.[25] This may explain why there is no manufacturing debris — if the flaking was done at the source, and the raw material was obtained from beach pebbles, the flaking areas are possibly now under water. The problem, then, is to explain the presence of so many hammerstones on Kartan sites. Perhaps the hammerstones were brought to resharpen blunted choppers.

The problem of the Kartan was tackled for his doctoral thesis by Lampert, who suggested that the Kartan belonged to the period 50–30,000 years ago and was the toolkit used by the first colonists. Lampert believes that Kangaroo Island was abandoned around 30,000 years ago, to be later reoccupied at the time of low sea level perhaps 18,000 years ago. The new occupants were not the users of the Kartan tools, but brought with them the technology which he found in the Seton rock shelter site — manufacturing small flint and quartz scrapers rather than the heavy quartzite choppers of the Kartan.

Lampert's argument for the Kartan being a particularly early assemblage appears to have been strengthened by the identification of 24 waisted tools from amongst the Kartan assemblages. Such tools have also been found in the Flinders Ranges and near Mackay in North Queensland. He suggests this tool type also formed a component of the earliest technology to arrive in Australia, but that it was later abandoned over most of the continent, since waisting was not necessary in a non-tropical environment. Similar waisted tools have been found at early sites in southeast Asia and in Papua-New Guinea. In this waisting, we may see a link with the grooved axes which have been found in northern Australia.[26]

Within the past few years, the Kartan has been identified in northeastern New South Wales at the Lime Springs site, where it is associated with the remains of the megafauna. There are some important implications for this finding. Indeed it needs to be clearly demonstrated that this is indeed the Kartan — some people defining the Kartan on the basis of its geographic distribution in South Australia. However, it does seem that the functional tools at the two locations are identical.[27]

Josephine Flood believes that the Kartan is indeed the earlier version of the core tool and scraper tradition. She sees Kangaroo Island and the surrounding coastal strip as being the only place where this early assemblage is preserved because:

- it is at sufficient altitude above present sea level

- it is close to the sea;

- it is close to Australia's largest river; and

- it is in an area with the greatest possible diversity of resources.

She believes it is 'among the few surviving remnants of Australia's continental shelf'.[28]

Edge-ground tools

Edge-grinding in Europe and the Middle East is always found associated with the Neolithic period and the beginnings of agriculture. Yet in Australia, Carmel Schrire (then Carmel White) excavated edge-ground axes, some of them grooved to indicate that they were hafted, buried in Arnhem Land deposits over 20,000 years old.[29] These were smaller than many later axeheads, and were manufactured by the pecking technique (hammer dressing). They were excavated at Nawamoyn dating between 21,000 and 25,000 years ago, and at Malangangerr dated to 23,000 years ago. Similar ground tools have been found in Japan at about the same age, and grooved and ground axeheads have been identified in Indochina 20,000 years ago and at Niah Cave in Sarawak 15,000 years ago. They appear to have a southeast Asian heritage.[30]

More recently, similar early axes have been found in the Kimberley and Cape York, where one has been suggested to have come from a deposit 31,000 years old!

There are two major questions which need to be addressed. What were they used for, and why were they not in use further south? Their restricted northerly distribution perhaps provides a clue to the answers of both of these questions. Assuming there was contact from north to south, and there almost certainly was, the function was one which was restricted to the tropical north.

There seems to have been an enormous diversity in Aboriginal technology prior to 30,000 years ago, with small flake tools in the southwest of Western Australia, giant Kartan tools on Kangaroo Island, edge-ground axes in the tropical north, and the core tool and scraper tradition along the lake shores of western New South Wales and in the woodlands of southeast Queensland.

Variations within the core tool and scraper tradition

The early assemblages of western New South Wales in places like Lake Mungo provided the basis on which the core tool and scraper tradition was built. It is often described in terms of the presumed functions of its components — this is particularly true of the term 'scraper', which applies to virtually anything with a retouched edge, regardless of whether it was actually used to scrape wood or any other substrate.[31]

Some prehistorians use the term 'chopper' to describe many of the bigger tools in this assemblage, although the term also has no real technological basis, since it depends on a presumed function. Josephine Flood says that 'Choppers are large heavy tools made from lumps of rock and they have a flaked cutting edge. They are used for heavy wood-working, such as chopping down trees'.[32]

Using Flood's definitions, the main characteristics of the Australian core tool and scraper tradition are 'the presence of large core tools, steep-edged, chunky high-backed scrapers, and concave, notched and "nosed" working edges. Flatter, convexed-edged and round scrapers also occur, which may have been used to make skins pliable for use as cloaks.' [33] Again this definition is less than perfect, for it includes an implied function for another class of flake tools. Perhaps, then, we should look at the two major components of these assemblages, and see what each really consists of.

Technically, a core tool is a tool that is made on a core. In other words, a piece of stone has first been used as a source of flakes, and then it has been used as a tool. Josephine Flood defines one type of 'core tool' in the following way: 'Some of them have a flat base, an overhanging, step-flaked edge and a high, domed shape like a horse's hoof, hence they have been called horsehoof cores.' [34]

The horsehoof core is a component of the Kartan industry. The distinction between Kartan and core tool and scraper horsehoof cores is based largely on size. Interestingly, Flood goes on to sugget that pebble tools 'have the same function as Mungo-type horsehoof cores'. [35] This leads us to the conclusion that the Kartan consists of horsehoof cores and pebble tools which have the same function as horsehoof cores. Now if we could only identify the function of horsehoof cores, we could explain the Kartan.

Unfortunately, not only can we not explain the function of horsehoof cores, but there is a great deal of scepticism as to whether they are tools at all. The kind of edge-damage which is found on many horsehoof cores is exactly the same kind of fine-edge damage as occurs when flakes are removed from a core. While it is clear that some horsehoof cores were used as tools, many may simply be discarded cores. The association of horsehoof cores and hammerstones may be the result of discard of the core and hammerstone and retention of the flakes!

Can a horsehoof core function as a 'chopper'? The short answer is yes, because it is technically possible for any sharp but thick edge to be used to chop or shave or plane wood. Whether or not this was the function of these tools will require extensive usewear studies, probably using microscopic analysis as well as replication studies. Even then it may not be possible to be confident about how horsehoof cores were used, in indeed they were used at all.

There are also problems associated with the 'scraper' component of the core tool and scraper tradition. Flood suggests that 'sturdy steep-edged flakes were also used for wood-working, such as scraping, sawing, incising and chiselling'. [36] Again we have a series of presumed functions, but this time replication studies conducted both in Australia and overseas tend to support the hypothesis that 'sturdy steep-edged flakes' were used as woodworking tools. [37] The pebble tools, horsehoof cores and scrapers are all woodworking tools. This suggests that wooden artefacts were being used which required stone tools for their manufacture.

At Wyrie Swamp in South Australia a series of wooden artefacts have been excavated from deposits dated at 10,000 years ago. The artefacts included barbed spears and boomerangs — exactly the kinds of wooden artefacts which would require the use of such stone tools for their manufacture and maintenance.

The notched and concave scrapers of the core tool and scraper tradition were probably used as spokeshaves for smoothing and sharpening spear shafts. There is some supportive evidence in the form of the art which is found in Arnhem Land dating back certainly before 5000 years ago, when boomerangs, barbed spears and other wooden artefacts were depicted.[38]

The Pleistocene stone tool industries in Australia seem to support the view that Aborigines were using stone tools primarily to manufacture a range of wooden tools, some of which may have been used for hunting. Other stone tools were possibly used to butcher game.

Hafting and the Australian small tool tradition

It was John Mulvaney who first suggested a simple technological basis for the distinction between the two stone traditions in Australia. He felt that the larger and earlier stone tools were probably all hand-held, and that the microlithic assemblages, including axes, adze flakes, points and small scrapers, were all hafted onto a handle.[39]

In the case of the axes, the purpose of the handle is obvious, and the dynamics of Australian edge-ground axes was studied in detail by Dickson.[40] In the case of the adze flakes, they were probably hafted onto the end of a handle, in the same way that tula adze flakes and probably elouera were end-hafted for woodworking to give greater leverage. Mulvaney believed that the microliths were used as spear points and barbs, and saw the analogy with the much-dreaded 'death spear' in southern New South Wales which was armed with one or two rows of stone chips. The advantage of this spear was that, even if the spear shaft fell out, the stone chips would remain inside, causing the animal (or person) to bleed profusely and eventually die.[41]

The discovery of flakes bearing gums and resins in earlier industries indicates that some hafting may have taken place during the Pleistocene, but the general thrust of Mulvaney's argument still has merit. Certainly the size and shape of many of the tools which are found in the Australian core tool and scraper tradition are suggestive of use while held in the hand, rather than by hafting. The widespread use of hafting may in itself have been a component of the technological innovations which accompanied the advent of the Australian small tool tradition.

On balance, the stone tool assemblages seem to indicate that a major technological change took place around 4000 years ago, associated with a greater use of hafted composite tools. Similar technological changes from large tools to smaller tools are recorded throughout the world. It is possible that the spearthrower was also first used at this time.

Hunting and intensification

The value in prehistory is not in the accumulation of data, but the interpretation of those data. Aboriginal people arrived in Australia, adapted to the new environment, adapted to changing environments, modified their technology, introduced the dingo, diversified and specialised across the landscape, and left their waste in campsites for archaeologists to discover. Having observed that these changes took place, it is necessary to discover why stone technology changed, why people moved into inhospitable areas like the sandy deserts, and why specialised economies developed along the coast.

A number of consistent patterns over time have been identified in the Australian archaeological record. The quantity discard rate of artefacts per site increased. It is apparent that in the pre-microlithic stone industries, the actual number of artefacts discarded per unit time (or per unit volume of excavated deposit) is small.

With the introduction of the small tool tradition, the discard rate of artefacts greatly increases, sometimes by a factor of ten, and occasionally by a factor of 100! Why so many stone flakes were being produced, and why there is an intensification in the rate of artefact production, requires explanation.[42]

The quantity of sites per unit area also increases dramatically, with many sites being occupied for the first time within the last 5000 years.[43]

Why do we find so many sites initially occupied only during the last 5000 years? Certainly stabilisation of the sea level may contribute to this process, but this does not satisfactorily explain why so many sites are first occupied during the last few thousand years. Why is there such an intensive use of some areas, particularly the coastal strip?

Associated with the technological changes, there are also changes in the spatial distribution of Aboriginal people. There is late movement into new areas like deserts, mountains and plains — areas previously considered too marginal to be used.

The model of desert colonisation proposed by Veth suggested that most parts of Australia were occupied by around 10,000 years ago, with the exception of the sandy deserts. Yet when Europeans arrived in Australia, Aboriginal people were successfully exploiting the entire continent, including difficult areas like the sandy deserts. The alpine areas of the Southern Highlands were being used, at least seasonally and probably year-round. Why would people colonise these inhospitable places?

Perhaps the answer lies in the adoption of the new technology — the introduction of small tool tradition. The changes from the core tool and scraper tradition which lasted until about 5000 years to the new Australian small tool technology are now well documented, but what is not clear is why the technology changed. After all, it had successfully enabled Aboriginal people to exploit the Australian environment for at least 40,000 years. Why change a successful technology?

The answer to this question may lie in the wider use of a range of smaller food resources which accompanied the new stone technology. Kangaroos, wallabies, possums, fish, eels and birds were all eaten more regularly in the last few thousand years.

In 1788 we find that Aborigines were exploiting a diverse range of small animals and plants — possums, fish, daisy yams, eels, rats, bandicoots, snakes, lizards and many more. Kangaroos, for which they had apparently developed a specialised hunting technology, and which would provide them with abundant meat, gradually became less important. Why did they eat poisonous plants like *Macrozamia*, which requires anything up to two weeks' preparation before it could be eaten?

All of these changes are components of the process referred to as 'intensification'. Perhaps one of the most interesting papers on the question of intensification was written by Lourandos.[44] Lourandos considers that intensification is a reflection of socioeconomic evolution, the changes over time which we can identify in the archaeological record. He sees two possible alternatives in trying to explain these changes — environmental/ecological and demographic models, and socially orientated explanatory frameworks.

Using his research on economic growth in southwest Victoria during the late Holocene, Lourandos suggested that it was the restructuring of social relationships which resulted in increased economic activity, which in turn resulted in complex social relations, economic growth, sedentism and population growth.

Lourandos sees Aboriginal people as controlling production by stabilising the resource yield and controlling regeneration of resources. This they can do by extending their ecological niche into marginal areas and using more efficient management techniques. He suggests that to interpret intensification, 'a wider approach needs to be introduced with an emphasis not on portable artefacts but on land and resource management strategies and their social implications'.[45]

He then suggests four characteristics or indicators of intensification:

- more intensive usage of individual sites;

- increased establishments of new sites;

- increased use of marginal environments; and

- increased complexity of site economy (that is, resource management strategy).

Lourandos' analysis confirms that new sites have been established at an increasing rate over the last 2000 years. The most complex sites are late in the sequence. For example, earth mounds and eel traps in western Victoria are less than 2500 years old.

Old sites are few and far between, Lourandos concludes, and the pattern he detected in Victoria is the same Australia-wide. He makes the important point that it is not just along the coast where these changes occur, but inland as well. This tends to weigh against the evidence of Lampert and Hughes that it is the stabilising sea levels during the mid-Holocene which enabled greater populations to be supported along the coastal strip.[46] Clearly if the intensification occurred in all environments it cannot be explained in simple terms like the stabilising of the sea level.

Lourandos looked at the ethnographic accounts of Aborigines in Victoria and suggested that the social patterns are as might be expected if the process of intensification was socially driven — that is, the economic patterns are the result of increasing social interactions.

Some of Lourandos' data were based on work in the northwestern Victorian mallee by Ross, who also found that there was greater use of the mallee during the late Holocene. She rejects the idea that climate alone caused the excursions into the mallee, as only the area immediately adjacent to the Murray River was in use until after 3500 years ago, after which more regular use was made of the arid areas. She therefore concludes that it was not climate (that is, rainfall or available water) that led people to use these resources — it was some other factor, and she believes this factor was an increasing Aboriginal population.[47]

Hughes and Lampert argued that there was a 'marked increase in population in coastal regions of southeastern Australia during the last 5000 years', based on new sites, intensity of site use, increased humanly caused sedimentation rates, and increased numbers of stone tools.[48] These changes were not sudden but gradual, but started about the time the small tool tradition was introduced, although there is some evidence to suggest that the changes had started slightly earlier in the Holocene.

Prehistoric change can be understood if it is based on the premise that a change in technology can be equated with a change in the resource base. Pre-microlithic assemblages are generalised, and probably reflect a low Aboriginal population density, with tool use restricted to woodworking and cutting. The core tool and scraper tradition assemblages have no specialised tools which are diagnostic of any particular economic specialisation. However, Australian backed blades of the small tool tradition can be compared with microlithic assemblages in other parts of the world, and in most cases such assemblages can be associated with either the hunting of small to medium sized animals or the harvesting of cereal crops.[49] Since there has been no evidence for cereal crops and sickle use amongst the Aborigines of Australia, it is not unreasonable to conjecture that the analogy holds true, and that Australian backed blades were used as projectile points and barbs for hunting small to medium sized animals, presumably macropods.

If this model of prehistoric change in Australia is correct, then within the last 4000 years the technological changes which are evident Australia-wide (with the exception of Tasmania) reflect a specialisation in hunting small to medium sized game. The technological innovations associated with the small tool tradition — including hafting of spear points and barbs, and probably the simultaneous introduction of the spearthrower — created the opportunity for a relatively narrow range of animals, particularly the kangaroos and wallabies, to be exploited more effectively and more efficiently. There is clearly a correlation between the new stone technology, increasing Aboriginal population density and greater social interaction. Lourandos argues that it was greater social interaction which resulted in technological change, but it seems more likely that the rapid and universal adoption of the new technology was intimately associated with increasing Aboriginal population densities.

If the interpretation of economic change and specialisation amongst the prehistoric Aboriginal population during the late Holocene is correct, then there are a number of indirect tests which can be used to confirm or reject the hypothesis that these changes were the result of an increasing population. Cohen proposed a number of indicators of population growth which could be investigated through careful analysis of the archaeological data.[50] If a significant proportion of these criteria are satisfied, he maintains that there is strong evidence for an increasing population. His indicators are:

1. PEOPLE ARE TRAVELLING INCREASING DISTANCES FOR FOOD.
   This is true for the collection of bogong moths in the Southern
   Highlands of New South Wales, bunya nuts in the Brisbane area
   and beached whales along the east coast.[51]

2. EXPANSION INTO NEW ECOLOGICAL ZONES.
   The sandy deserts are occupied relatively late in the sequence,
   and within the Sydney region Blue Mountains are occupied on a
   permanent basis for the first time during the late Holocene, so
   this agrees with the model of increasing population.

3. INCREASED EXPLOITATION OF MICRONICHES.
   The intensive use of the woodland resources on the coastal plains
   fulfils this criterion.[52]

4. REDUCED SELECTIVITY IN FOODS EATEN, FULLER UTILISATION OF ALL
   RESOURCES.
   There can be little doubt that a Holocene increase in the
   exploitation of shellfish, possums and tuberous and toxic plant
   foods satisfy this requirement.

5. INCREASE IN USE OF WATER-BASED RESOURCES (EG, SHELLFISH).
   This appears to be true, although there is some doubt as to the
   degree of shellfish exploitation prior to the advent of the
   microlithic industry.

6. SHIFT FROM EATING LARGE MAMMALS TO SMALL MAMMALS, BIRDS AND
   REPTILES.
   This certainly appears to be true late in the Holocene, with
   possums replacing macropodids as a major component of the diet.

7. CONSUMPTION OF ORGANISMS AT LOWER TROPHIC LEVELS.
   The concentration on yams and other plant foods agrees with this
   prediction.

8. USE OF FOODS REQUIRING A GREAT DEAL OF PREPARATION.
   Macrozamia exploitation could fulfil this requirement, as suggested by Beaton.[53] Many other plants used by Aboriginal people
   required treatment to remove toxins.

9. ENVIRONMENTAL DEGRADATION VIA THE USE OF FIRE.
   This seems likely in the Sydney region, based on the evident of
   Hughes and Sullivan.[54]

10. SKELETAL EVIDENCE OF INCREASING MALNUTRITION THROUGH TIME.
    Aboriginal skeletal remains from the Murray Valley show increas-
    ing evidence of environmental stress over time.[55]

11. EXPLOITATION OF SMALLER INDIVIDUALS WITHIN A SPECIES.
    Such evidence can be found in the archaeological record from a
    range of coastal shell middens and from inland rock shelters.

12. EXPLOITED SPECIES DISAPPEAR FROM THE ARCHAEOLOGICAL RECORD.
    Many shell middens in southeastern Australia show a change in
    species composition over time, with some species disappearing
    altogether from the upper levels.[56]

13. SCARCITY OF RESOURCES.
    The loss of access to sources of stone in the Sydney region and
    the greater curation of stone tools in other parts of Australia
    appear to fit this pattern.[57]

14. SEDENTISM.
    There are certainly indications of increased sedentism, particu-
    larly along the coast, with descriptions of villages at Botany Bay
    and the discovery of stone foundations in Victoria.[58]

Of the fourteen indicators suggested by Cohen, all appear to apply in
certain parts of Australia during the late Holocene. Cohen points out
that it may seem paradoxical that population pressure can be cited as
the basis for both sedentism and seasonal transhumanance. However,
it is possible for populations to exploit particular areas intensively
but retain the capacity to travel large distances when other resources
become abundant.

The evidence seems clear enough. Aboriginal populations in
Australia increased significantly during the last 5000 years, and
along with the population increase came a far greater use of some
specific resources, notably kangaroos and wallabies, plant foods and
shellfish. Ethnographic evidence suggests that the spread of edge-
ground axes into southern Australia may have been associated with
an increased exploitation of possums and other tree-dwelling animals.
For any given species of animal which was being hunted by
Aborigines during the Holocene, the predator population increased,
the efficiency of hunting improved due to technological change, and
if Aboriginal burning also increased, then the habitat could also have
been changed. All of these factors would have impacted on the prey
populations and ultimately on the predators the Aboriginal people.

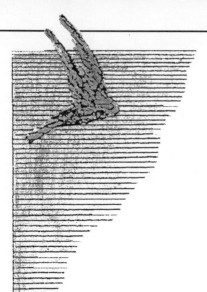

CHAPTER 7

Prehistoric population density

In attempting to identify the nature and extent of Aboriginal environmental impacts within Australia, the Aboriginal population density is a major contributing factor. In recent years it has become increasingly obvious that the number of Aboriginal people living in Australia in the late eighteenth century had been grossly underestimated.

In 1930, Professor Radcliffe-Brown suggested that the total Aboriginal population of Australia when European settlement began in 1788 was approximately 300,000 people.[1] This figure was accepted almost without question for the next 50 years. By the early 1980s, the archaeological evidence was beginning to accumulate, and it was presenting data indicating that the contact Aboriginal population may have been considerably greater.

In 1983, Noel Butlin from the Australian National University published a book called *Our Original Aggression*, in which he estimated the population of southeastern Australia to have been greater than 1 million, and suggested that the total Australia wide population may have been close to 2 million.[2] His work was based on birth and death rates of Aborigines in Victoria, and he claimed that 90% of the Australian Aboriginal population was dead by 1850. Butlin argued that introduced diseases such as smallpox, syphilis, tuberculosis and measles totally devastated the Aboriginal populations of eastern Australia — populations which had no resistance to these European diseases. Can these figures be supported by other ethnographic data?

One area where it may be possible to assess the accuracy of Butlin's estimates is in the Sydney region.

An ethnographic reconstruction of the western Cumberland Plain confirmed a relatively high Aboriginal population density at contact, with the 600 square km survey area supporting between five and eight clans, each consisting of approximately 50 people, an overall minimum population density of around 0.5 persons per square km. For the coastal strip around Sydney in 1788, Governor Phillip estimated that the total population was 1500. The population between Botany Bay and Broken Bay of 1500 persons was supported by later reconstructions, and this represents a coastal population density of approximately 1.2 persons per squre km. The total population of the Sydney region, including the Hawkesbury River and the lower Blue Mountains, was probably between 4000 and 8000.[3]

Other ethnographic reconstructions have been carried out, and these give similar values. Lourandos reported a population density of 0.3–0.4 persons per square km for inland Aborigines in southwest Victoria, and 0.4–0.7 persons per square km for coastal Aborigines in the same region.[4] The estimated population densities for both the western Cumberland Plain and the coastal strip around Sydney are slightly higher than the figures cited by Lourandos, but in view of the depopulation which followed the smallpox epidemic and the relatively late acquisition of the ethnographic data from southwest Victoria, the figures are not unreasonable.

Indeed, there is strong evidence to support a high Aboriginal population density at contact. In general terms, we can probably interpret the term 'intensification' as relating to increasing population density, but associated with new and varied technology and exploitation of lower trophic level resources, in some cases requiring a specialised technology. One consequence of these changes is that there were also concurrent or consequent changes in social interactions between groups.[5]

What was the social organisation like over the first 50,000 years of Aboriginal occupation of Australia? In reality, we have little idea what the structure of Aboriginal social groups was like for those years. The relatively sparse scatter of stone artefacts, and the paucity of faunal remains, allow speculation and little more. All we can really say is that during the Pleistocene the band size was probably relatively small, perhaps in the order of twenty people, and the population density was relatively low compared with population densities at the time of European settlement. It also seems likely that people were largely restricted to the better environments along the coasts and adjacent to the major rivers and lakes.

With the advent of the small tool tradition we find an increase in the amount of stone discarded over time, as well as an increase in the number of sites being occupied. On the surface, this looks like strong evidence for an increasing population, but perhaps a few words of caution are necessary.

In order to produce a single functional hand-held stone scraper, you may produce ten waste flakes. In order to make one Bondi point, the stone reduction process may result in 100 waste flakes. Yet you may require six or eight Bondi points to barb a single spear, and you will still need the scraper (or its equivalent) to make the spear shaft. Perhaps we need to take care when we make the jump between numbers of artefacts and population. It is also worth considering the fact that there is a reduction in the amount of stone recovered from the most recent levels of many sites, particularly those along the coast.[6] Does this mean the population was low? Clearly it was not, as ethnographic accounts confirm.

A second point relates to the number of sites first being occupied. Let us assume we have twenty people who occupy a single site. They have a domestic dispute, and break into three groups. There are instantaneously three times as many sites being produced by the same number of people. Or perhaps our twenty people, who always camped at one site and foraged around that site, suddenly decided that they liked to eat fish on Friday, yams on Monday and possums on Wednesday, and that they would spend the weekend camped close to their relatives. If these resources are available in different parts of the clan estate, we now have four camp sites in a week, where before we had one. Certainly, increasing numbers of sites is a clear indication of changing settlement patterns, but not *necessarily* an indication of increasing populations. However, over the long time span (4000 years) associated with the Australian small tool tradition, it is almost certain that these changes in settlement pattern were indeed accompanied by increasing Aboriginal populations.

When Europeans arrived in Australia they found Aboriginal people divided into over 600 language groups. Within some of these language groups different dialects were spoken. Within the dialect groups were distinct clans, or landowning groups. Within each clan, or sometimes overlapping between clans, were bands — groups which often foraged together as a unit — and within each band there were generally two or three family units. Depending on the circumstances, combinations of most of these groups could be gathered at the one spot. Certainly family groups are likely to have foraged individually during the winter months. In the summer, a band or clan may come together and camp at the one spot (these are almost certainly the groups who occupied the 'villages'). At times, we know that groups which consisted of individuals from several linguistic tribes would come together — particularly during ceremonial occasions.

Which of these social groups leaves its imprint in the archaeological record? In simple terms, all of them do, as well as individuals who may be carrying out a specific activity. However, the archaeological visibility of a site need not bear any relationship to the number of people present. For example, at an initiation ceremony there may be hundreds of people present, but few stone artefacts or other cultural remains will be discarded.

Meehan's study of shellfish gathering amongst the Anbarra people of Arnhem Land gives us many insights into the number of people who participate in various events, and the subsequent site visibility.[7] Her work amongst the Burrara language group, Gidjingali dialect (400 speakers), Anbarra people, who included members of six different clans, suggested that their population density overall was about 0.5 people per square km, which is in general agreement with the Victorian and Sydney data. She suggests that these people occupied both home base camps and dinner-time camps, often with scatters of shellfish remaining as the only trace of their existence. She documents groups ranging from individuals to one gathering of over 300 at a 'kunapipi' ceremony. There were four seasonal movements to home-base camps, and at each of these areas there were up to three different 'sites'. The mean number of people at a 'site' was around 40.

On the basis of her results, Meehan calculated the number of people present at a number of significant archaeological sites with large accumulations of shell midden. For the Richmond River middens in northern New South Wales, she estimated a population of 35. At West Point in Tasmania, the figure is about 40 people. Both of these compare favourably with the 'real' number of Anbarra people. She also quotes data from Tasmania, where a French expedition encountered 48 Aborigines gathering, cooking and eating abalone. The historical observations of group size seem to roughly correspond with the contemporary community size in Arnhem Land. However, shellfish contribute only around 5% by weight of their diet. Yet shellfish are clearly the most obvious and important archaeological data we find in coastal sites.

Meehan also quotes population densities for Central Australia of 1 person per 250 square km. This demonstrates that there existed a tremendous variability across the continent, corresponding to the variability of environments. In most cases the population density can be related to the availability of water and biological productivity. The drier the environment the fewer people it can support. It is apparent that there is no average figure which can be applied to Aboriginal populations in the ethnographic present. Similarly it would be presumptuous to try to estimate the average size of a group in the prehistoric period, unless attention is paid to the local environmental factors like water and productivity.

Perhaps the way of approaching the question of increasing Aboriginal populations is to ask: If not increasing populations, what has resulted in the intensification? Lourandos would argue social interactions, but others would argue new technology. It would seem that the crucial question is how and why did the small tool tradition arrive in Australia, and why was it adopted so widely and so rapidly? It is probable that it was adopted because it made life easier — it enabled more efficient exploitation of resources. This in turn led to increased population densities, which in turn resulted in changing social patterns.

If there was such a large population, and the need for more food, why did Aborigines not practise some form of agriculture? If we compare Australia with Papua-New Guinea, Polynesia, New Zealand and South-East Asia, we find that, rather than being suitable for the culture of a few specific staples (like taro or sweet potato), Australia had a naturally occurring diversity of plant resources which was easier and more reliable to exploit if not planted as a monoculture. Perhaps Aborigines are best looked upon as polyculturalists, using fire, social prohibitions, and replanting of parts of plants (e.g., yams) in order to exploit these resources most effectively.[8]

The social system which was in operation was clearly not flexible enough to accommodate the mass arrival of Europeans. If we accept that there was a substantial (and increasing) Aboriginal population, tightly organised and with relatively little 'free' or available space between clan territories, it is apparent why the European economic system could not coexist with the Aboriginal system. The available resources, in terms of a hunter-gatherer economy, were already utilised to the fullest extent. Only by degrading the existing ecosystem was the European population able to survive — and this of course was at the expense of the Aboriginal system.

When examining the distribution of sites across the landscape, or excavating a site, what prehistorians are trying to do is to understand the processes which have led to the distribution of these sites, and to explain the contents of each site. They are trying to reconstruct the way of life of the Aboriginal people who created these imprints on the landscape. Based on the archaeological data, it is possible to speculate about the number of people, their social organisation, and perhaps their patterns of interaction. If we detect changes in the archaeological record, then these changes must reflect the activities of Aborigines in the past. If we can predict the location of sites, or the age of a particular assemblage, or the likely number of people who were camped on a site, we have succeeded. So let us take the final step. If we have detected all of these changes on the mainland, what would we expect to happen in Tasmania, where there seems to have been a relatively small population, completely isolated from the technological changes which were taking place on the mainland after 8000 years ago? There was no small tool tradition in Tasmania, no dingo, no spearthrower, and no edge-ground axe. So what kinds of social and population changes would be detectable in the Tasmanian archaeological record?

Jones estimated the Tasmanian population to be in the order of 3–4000 at contact.[9] At first glance this appears to be too low for such a large island, but it is worth remembering that the climate was inhospitable on the west coast, and much of the southwest was impenetrable scrub. In fact only a small proportion of the landscape was efficiently used. Would this have been different if the small tool tradition had become established in Tasmania? We know that Tasmanians used fire to open up the landscape, and the timing of this phenomenon is interesting — about 4000 years ago, the time when the small tool tradition was spreading across the mainland, and a time when fish were suddenly abandoned as a food source.[10] We see some close parallels between the mainland and Tasmania. We see a greater reliance on terrestrial animals; a greater spread of raw materials, with some sources of stone being transported over 80 km; we see coastal populations apparently moving away from the coast, perhaps seasonally; we see off-shore islands like Hunter Island being used for the first time since they were part of the mainland. In short, we see the same changes in settlement patterns and presumably social organisation which were taking place on the mainland, even though there was no contact across Bass Strait. This strongly suggests that the pressures which were causing change on the mainland were probably also acting on the Tasmanian Aborigines. If this is the case, we cannot explain the process simply in terms of the introduction of new technology, because in Tasmania there was no new technology.

If intensification is indeed detectable in the archaeological record of Tasmania, it perhaps supports Lourandos' argument that it is social change which leads and technological change which follows, but it could equally well indicate that the Tasmanian population was increasing at the same time as the mainland population.

The final question we should ask ourselves is where was Aboriginal culture headed when Europeans arrived? Would Aborigines have followed the pattern evident in much of the world, and develop agriculture in order to support the growing population? Most prehistorians would argue strongly that they would not have. They had no suitable animals to domesticate. This of course did not stop the development of agricultural practices perhaps 10,000 years ago in Papua-New Guinea, but this obviously was not an appropriate economic system for Australia, with its highly variable and unpredictable rainfall.[11] It is better to argue that the hunter-gatherer system was most appropriate for the Australian environment, which was precisely why it had lasted so long, adapting and evolving as the population increased. The social system, with all its religious and mythological trappings, had evolved to ensure that the Aborigines most effectively exploited their environment. Within the limits of their technology, that is precisely what they were doing were Europeans arrived in 1788.

The dingo

One change which occurred in the Australian environment, and which can be firmly associated with Aboriginal people, is the arrival and subsequent spread of the dingo. The date of its arrival in Australia can be estimated both directly and indirectly. Archaeological evidence shows that it was established in parts of Australia by 3–3500 years ago.[12] However, there are no dingoes in Tasmania or in Papua-New Guinea, suggesting it arrived after the rising seas had cut off these two islands from the mainland. That means they arrived sometime after 6–8000 years ago, when sea levels stabilised, and it probably first landed in the north.

The distances between the islands to the north of Australia and the mainland provide strong evidence as to how it arrived — it came in a canoe or on a raft. It would be highly unlikely that a dingo could otherwise survive an ocean crossing of such distances.

Based on its reproductive rate and the capacity to travel large distances relatively quickly, it probably took less than 500 years for them to occupy the entire continent. It may have been dispersed intentionally, for, if the ancestral dingo was domesticated when it came, pups could have been traded from tribe to tribe.

Biological data on the dingo demonstrates some interesting facts. They breed only once a year (domestic dogs can breed twice) and their numbers tend to remain constant. If the population increases the number of breeding females decreases. Their ancestors may have been found on the Indian subcontinent. Traders may have reached

Timor bringing various animals with them, and it has been suggested that this may also explain the origins of the small tool tradition. It has many similarities with stone assemblages from India.[13]

The dingo is a highly adaptable animal, and by the time Europeans arrived in Australia it was found in alpine country like the Snowy Mountains, in the deserts of Central Australia, in the forests of the Great Dividing Range and in the widespread woodlands. Dingoes tend to be bigger in the west and smaller in the east, and there are varying colour varieties, from the common reddish brown to black to the alpine variety which is white with thick fur.

Aboriginal people used the dingoes in a number of ways. They were pets, blankets, hunting aids and food. Other than man, they had few predators, but juvenile animals were eaten by eagles and possibly large snakes and goannas.

The fact that Tasmania did not have any dingoes before European settlement did not stop Tasmanian Aborigines acquiring dogs, and in particular greyhounds, for hunting after white settlements were established. Dogs have been blamed for the extinction of the Tasmanian emu by 1850.[14]

Prey

A wild dingo will eat a broad range of prey, but the preferred food are animals in the range of 10–20 kg. Alternation of food supply is a common trait exhibited by dingoes when a particular resource becomes scarce. They do not fit the conventional predator-prey models because they can use a diverse range of foods, rather like humans. A dingo can reduce the population of a prey species without itself being reduced, provided there are other species available to eat.[15] Popular prey animals include swamp wallabies, ned-necked wallabies, wombats, brush-tail possums, ring-tail possums, rats, birds, bandicoots, and even ducks and geese. Juvenile kangaroos are common food items, particularly pouched young and immature females.[16]

Studies have shown that an increase in the dingo population leads to an increase in large prey exploitation. However, a study of the effects of a major fire at Nadgee Nature Reserve on the New South Wales south coast demonstrated that dingoes will essentially eat whatever food is available. Large animals were hunted when small animals were scarce.[17]

Dingo predation on kangaroos and wallabies can disrupt the normal breeding patterns. Wallabies breed year round under heavy hunting pressure, but stress can cause the ejection of pouched young.[18]

Population densities of prey animals on both sides of the dingo proof fence which runs across South Australia and into Queensland differ enormously. Where no dingoes were found, red kangaroo numbers were increased 166 times, and emu numbers were twenty times higher.[19]

Dingoes kill more animals than they can eat, killing on average 0.38 kg of prey per kg dingo weight per day. This is a very high ratio. They also have the ability to hunt in groups (pack hunting) when numbers are high, and can therefore kill larger animals. As the dingo population increases there is also more efficient use of each kill, and not necessarily more prey species killed.[20]

It has also been observed that grey kangaroos spend their time more in groups if dingoes are hunting them. This may make them easier for Aborigines to hunt. Other studies suggest that the removal of the dingo may lead to an increase in koala populations, implying that koala populations in the past were kept low by dingo predation.[21] Certainly koalas are not self-regulating, and they may outstrip the food resources and become locally extinct if the population is not kept in check by hunting.

Competition

When the dingo arrived in Australia, there were already two medium to large sized carnivores present — the thylacine or Tasmanian tiger, and *Sarcophilus*, or Tasmanian devil. It is widely accepted that the dingo was a more efficient carnivore, a faster breeder, and therefore drove the thylacine to extinction on the mainland.[22]

The thylacine had a reproductive rate of two to four offspring per year, and they probably bred only once per year. Evidence from Tasmania in the nineteenth century suggests that thylacines could kill dogs, and presumably also dingoes. Interestingly, the most recent date for thylacines on the mainland, 2200 years ago, is associated with dingo remains.[23]

There was another potential competitor for the thylacine — man. Aborigines seem to have begun intensively exploiting small to medium sized game within the last 4000 years, perhaps to the detriment of the thylacine. Possibly the combination of increasing Aboriginal populations, in addition to the dingo, caused the animal to be outcompeted. Aborigines were known to have eaten thylacines in Tasmania, and on the mainland they certainly made necklaces out of *Sarcophilus* teeth — one necklace required 47 individual devils![24]

The evidence from Riversleigh fossil beds in Queensland suggests a gradual decline in the diversity of the thylacinids. There were only two species by 15 million years ago, and one species by 8 million years ago. However, if a species survived without change for the last 8 million years, it must have been well adapted to its environment.[25]

Perhaps the reason that the *Sarcophilus* survived longer on the mainland, and continues to flourish in Tasmania, is that it is a scavenger, and because dingoes overkill, there may have been an increase in the amount of food available to the devil once dingoes became established.

It seems likely that dingoes competed with Aborigines directly, exploiting the same food like wallabies and kangaroos. It is possible then that the presence of the dingo contributed to the need for Aborigines to exploit smaller resources.

The dingo directly or indirectly caused the extinction of the thylacine and the devil on the mainland; competed directly with Aborigines for small to medium game; kept the numbers of some animal species down; and may well have introduced new diseases into Australia.

Clearly, the arrival of the dingo had a major and direct impact on at least some animal species, and almost certainly had indirect impacts on others. Because Aboriginal people brought the dingo to Australia, they are indirectly responsible for the changes which resulted from their actions.

One of the species which was indirectly impacted by the dingo was man. The dingo was a direct competitor, consuming the same kinds of prey species as Aboriginal people. So at the same time as the Aboriginal population was increasing, the dingo was reducing the availability of some animal foods. With the increased stress on the kangaroos, wallabies, wombats, possums and koalas, which were hunted by both dingoes and Aborigines, it becomes increasingly important to understand how many animals could actually be hunted before there was a significant decline in the prey populations.

How many roos can a roo-shooter shoot and still have roos to shoot?

The level of sustainable harvesting rates is what needs to be characterised. John Winter from the Zoology Department of the University of Queensland looked at this question in 1970. Winter's paper was aimed at trying to answer the question posed in the title, specifically: what is the sustainable harvesting rate of kangaroos in Queensland? Between 1964 and 1969, almost 6 million kangaroos were shot in Queensland by professional shooters. Conservationists were concerned that this would wipe out kangaroos altogether. The official

Queensland government policy was that the level of hunting would not cause any significant reduction in the numbers of kangaroos. Who was correct? Winter approached the problem in a scientific manner. He argued, correctly, that what both conservationists and the government wanted was to maintain a stable kangaroo population and that, in order to achieve this only the surplus animals should be harvested. To calculate the excess, it is necessary to know the existing population size and the breeding rate. Winter attempted to determine the size of the population that could sustain a given rate of harvesting without endangering that population.[26]

To calculate this, the following information was required:

- the number of joeys born to a female in a year;

- the proportion of females giving birth to a joey each year;

- the age at which juveniles (particularly females) mature;

- the sex ratio of the population;

- the natural mortality of the joey; and

- mortality of the juvenile age classes.

Winter combined the biological data for red and grey kangaroos and came up with the following model. The data for red and grey kangaroos was combined in such a way that the optimum rate was used. The only major difference was in the juvenile death rate of the red kangaroo, which is highly variable and can be influenced by drought. Working with a stable hypothetical population of 375 animals, he demonstrated that the harvesting rate to maintain a stable population is 15%.

There are three categories in the population — adults, joeys and juveniles, and as one batch of joeys becomes juvenile it is replaced by another batch of joeys. In a year, 100 females give birth to 50 male and 50 female joeys. Because 25% of the joeys die, 37.5 individuals of each sex survive to become juveniles in the following year. Similarly, 25% of the juveniles die, so 28 of each sex survive to become adults the following year. With 56 adults being added to the population annually, 56 adults can be removed annually without altering the number of animals in the population. This surplus of adults represents 15% of the population, which may be removed either by natural mortality, shooting or migration. These are obviously crude estimates, but they clearly demonstrate that the maximum harvesting rate is in the order of 15%.

On the basis of his model, it is allowable to shoot 1 in every 6.5 kangaroos per year in an given area. The critical question then is what is the total kangaroo population of that area? Density figures for different locations vary enormously, but published densities range from 0.6–0.75 per square km in the Macdonnel Ranges in the Northern Territory up to 3.5 per square km in Wilcannia in western New South Wales. For southeast Queensland, the estimated average population density used by Winter was 1–2 kangaroos per square km.[27]

In 1965, 1.1 million kangaroos were shot in Queensland. To support this rate, the average kangaroo population density would have to have been about 4.5 per square km — higher than any rate which had been recorded. However, hunting was not evenly distributed across the state and in the Roma area, for example, based on the harvesting rates, the population would need to have been around 35 kangaroos per square km to support that level of hunting. Winter demonstrated quite clearly that the harvesting rates in Queensland were far too high.

Where does all of this lead to when it comes to the impact Aborigines may have had on kangaroos? After all, people as eminent as Frith and Calaby, in their famous book on kangaroos, have said: 'Before European settlement, Aborigines with their primitive weapons preyed on kangaroos but there were never a great number of Aborigines in the whole continent and it is difficult to imagine them being a very serious danger.'[28]

This statement needs more careful consideration. Firstly, were Aboriginal weapons primitive? This is doubtful. With the use of spearthrowers, stone-tipped and barbed spears, and fire to drive kangaroos, it was probably a very efficient technology.

Secondly, were there really 'never a great number of Aborigines in the whole continent'? The Aboriginal population densities calculated for various parts of Australia suggest that population densities greater than 1 person per 2 square km were typical in the southeast of the continent and also in the tropical north. If we focus on the Sydney region, the earliest population estimate was made by Governor Phillip, who suggested that there were 1500 Aborigines on the coast between Botany Bay and Broken Bay. This suggests that the entire Cumberland Plain probably supported a substantially larger population.

Butlin suggests that the Aboriginal population in 1788 was 1–2 million.[29] For the Cumberland Plain, he estimates a population of 4000. Other estimates would indicate that this is too low, so let us accept for the sake of argument that the total population of the Cumberland Plain falls within the range of 3500 to 7000 people in 1788.[30]

If we accept that the kangaroo population has almost certainly increased since Europeans arrived, mainly through the provision of

more watering points and grass through clearing, then we would be
generous in assuming that the kangaroo population on the
Cumberland Plain in 1788 was 1–2 per square km, the same density
as in southeast Queensland. The area of the Cumberland Plain is
around 7000 square km, so the total kangaroo population would have
been between 7000 and 14,000. In round figures, if Aborigines killed
15% of the population per year, which would maintain a stable population, then the maximum total number of kangaroos which could be
killed per year is between 1000 and 2000.

If the Aboriginal population of the Cumberland Plain was somewhere between 3500 and 7000, of whom say 30% were hunters
(excluding women and children), then there were between 1000 and
2000 hunters. In other words, if each hunter killed one kangaroo per
year, the population would remain in balance, but if a hunter killed
any more than one per year, there would be a decline in the kangaroo
population. Indeed, if each hunter killed two kangaroos per year, kangaroos would become extinct on the Cumberland Plain in less than
ten years! Clearly, that couldn't happen, because fewer kangaroos
would be killed as the population fell, but there is an important point
to be made here. It is not that the Aborigines could cause the extinction of kangaroos, even though mathematically it would be possible.
Rather it is the fact that kangaroos simply could not provide a significant proportion of protein in the diet of Aborigines in the Cumberland
Plain, because of the relatively high number of Aborigines and the
relatively low numbers of kangaroos.

There are two aspects of this conclusion which I want to investigate a little further. The first is: if this was the situation on the
Cumberland Plain, was it also the situation elsewhere in Australia?
This is not an easy question to answer, but again, if we use Butlin's
population estimates for various parts of Australia, and taking into
account the variation in kangaroo densities which relate to climatic
variability, the chances are that the same level of predator–prey relationship existed everywhere. If this is so, then the conclusion is that it
was Aboriginal hunting which controlled the population density of
kangaroos. The significance of this becomes even more apparent if we
remember that large animals, including both kangaroos and
Aborigines, are tied to water, so there will be a clustered distribution
in the semi-arid and arid zones.

The second aspect I wish to pursue is: if this was the case with
kangaroos, could it also be the case with other animal species? I sus-
pect that the answer is yes for some species but no for many others.
The attraction of the kangaroos, and to a lesser extent large wallabies,
is that they provide a large amount of protein for every animal killed.

All other extant terrestrial Australian animals are smaller and would therefore provide less food per unit capture effort. However, the same cannot be said for some marine animals. Seals, dugongs and perhaps turtles would be selectively hunted for the same reasons as kangaroos, providing adequate canoes or rafts were available. It is interesting to speculate whether the restriction in the distribution of dugongs from the Sydney area may be related to this fact. The seagrass beds in Botany Bay would have been an ideal dugong grazing area, and dugong remains have been found in Aboriginal sites, but no European has ever seen a dugong in Botany Bay.[31]

It also seems likely that Aborigines intentionally modified the environment to maximise the kangaroo populations (among other things) by regular low-intensity burning of the sclerophyll forests and woodlands.[32] We know that the microlithic hunting technologies which existed until around 2000 years ago all over Australia did not survive. There is strong direct and indirect evidence that kangaroos were overexploited, causing a reduction in their numbers to the point where other food sources were exploited, requiring the adoption of other technologies. This would explain the expansion of various fishing technologies along the east coast within the last 1–2000 years; the acquisition of the edge-ground hatchet for hunting possums in southern Australia; the use of cooperative techniques associated with building fish traps, eel farming, and kangaroo drives; and sharing rich resources like stranded whales, bunya nuts, bogong moths and burrawang seeds. And remember, at about the same time that Aboriginal people were specialising on kangaroos a new predator was introduced into Australia — the dingo, a predator which was particularly successful at hunting kangaroos after fire, and which killed more than it could eat.

The question which follows on from all of this is of course: did Aborigines cause the extinction of the megafauna after all? Couldn't we use the same logic to suggest that the large animals were hunted to extinction, or at least to a very low level. There are several important factors which must be kept in mind. The Aboriginal population density at the time the megafauna became extinct was almost certainly much lower than 2000 years ago, and the technology which was available to hunt the megafauna is likely to have been less effective, and certainly inferior to that which involved barbed spears, woomeras and controlled fires. There were no dingoes in Australia when the megafauna became extinct, and they probably had no major predators. Were they the naive fauna which simply waited to be killed? No. Any animal population which is hunted will very quickly learn to avoid humans — there are many examples of this from all over the world and in many different parts of the animal kingdom. It was climate that made the difference, and the Aboriginal people perhaps took advantage of the fact that the megafauna became restricted to the better watered areas and may well have applied the *coup de grâce*.[33]

This does not imply that Aboriginal impacts could not have caused any extinctions. Some animals were restricted to narrow habitats. Some terrestrial animals probably could not adapt to the introduction of frequent Aboriginal fires, particularly in environmentally sensitive areas like the semi-arid zone. In the same way that some animals became extinct where Aboriginal burning stopped, some animals probably became extinct, or at least more restricted in their distribution, when intensive Aboriginal burning was initiated, perhaps 4000 years ago.

What can be observed in the late Holocene archaeological record is a shift from large animals to smaller animals. It is unlikely that possums would be disadvantaged by Aboriginal mosaic burning. Possums could survive low-intensity fires, and would probably be better off with new shoots and perhaps more nesting sites. Indeed, the cessation of Aboriginal burning may have adversely effected possums. It would be interesting to compare two similar areas — one which is still being burned by Aboriginal people and one which is not — to see what the impact of traditional burning practices is on small to medium sized arboreal and terrestrial mammals.[34]

What our manipulation of Winter's model has shown is that it is possible to model the impact of Aborigines on at least some animal populations. We can show that Aborigines certainly *could* have impacted on kangaroo population density. Archaeology tells us that Aborigines did change their technologies. Palaeontologists can show us that the distribution and abundance of some mammal species did change during the late Holocene.

At the time of European settlement many observers — including the famous explorers like Mitchell, Oxley and Sturt — all reported that the open environment in the relatively flat country in western New South Wales was maintained by Aboriginal burning, and this almost certainly had an impact on the flooding regimes of the Murray–Darling River system. It is interesting to speculate whether or not some of the salinity problems which European farmers are now facing in the Murrumbidgee and Murray River systems may not have originated well before Europeans reached the area. Field studies along these lines may help to answer this question.

There is some indirect evidence to suggest that in areas like the north side of the Hawkesbury River, fires may have become less frequent within the last 1000 years, with the fauna being exploited changing from open woodland species to wet sclerophyll and rainforest species, perhaps suggesting that there weren't enough kangaroos to hunt so burning stopped as the rainforest resources became more valuable.[35]

However we interpret the data, it seems clear that Aboriginal people did modify the vegetation, did have an impact on some animal species directly, and did change the species they were eating and the technology they were using to exploit those species. All of these things took place while the Aboriginal population continued to grow. These processes and developments were still taking place in 1788, when Europeans changed the direction of Aboriginal population growth from an upwards curve to a downwards one.

By 1791, a significant proportion — probably between 50% and 90% — of the Aborigines in the Sydney area had died. In other parts of the southeast, the same pattern occurred. By around 1800, the vast majority of Aborigines in southeastern Australia were dead. Indeed by 1840 there were probably only 300 (5% or less) of the original population still living in the Sydney area.[36]

One implication is that traditional Aboriginal social structure was *never* seen by Europeans except for the first eighteen months in Sydney. Even here, the Europeans had not travelled more than about 40 km from the coast, and contacts with the Aborigines were rare. Any interpretation of traditional lifestyles is warped by the massive depopulations which took place, and as a result we must always interpret ethnographic data with extreme caution. What is recorded by ethnographers is never 'traditional' in the pre-European sense of the word.

Changes in the physical environment

Having looked at some of the changes which took place in Australia during the late Holocene, including technological and biological ones, it is then necessary to look at the hard evidence for changes in the landscape — particularly in terms of land degradation or destabilisation. What is the evidence that Aborigines actually had the capacity to modify the physical as well as the biological landscape?

In southwestern Victoria, Lourandos found evidence for Aborigines digging elaborate channels, connecting swamps, and therefore increasing the productivity of the area for eels. It may not be too far from the truth to consider this as eel farming. The channels at Toolondo were mechanically created, dug with human hands, or more likely with digging sticks.[37]

The channels have been described by Flood in the following terms:

Artificial channels 400 metres long were dug out with digging sticks to join two swamps, 2.5 km apart, in different drainage systems. They were separated by a low divide, which was cut through to allow water to flow in either direction. Eels were thus able to extend their range and increase in number, and the channels made it easy to catch them… It was estimated that 3000 cubic metres of earth was dug out of the Toolondo complex, a remarkable feat implying a high degree of organisation.[38]

Flood also gives a good description of similar structures at Lake Condah, one of several locations where they have been identified:

stone races, canals, traps and stone walls. The races were constructed by building walls from broken blocks of the black volcanic rock that litters the Lake Condah region. These walls were up to a metre in height and width and more than 50 metres long. In some places, canals up to a metre in depth and as much as 300 metres in length were dug into basalt bedrock by removing loose and broken rocks… The sophisticated network was so cunningly designed that it took advantage of both rising and falling water. Traps were built at different levels and, as the lake rose or fell, different traps came into operation progressively.[39]

This type of large-scale land modification does not appear to have a precedent in Australia — suggesting that moving large quantities of earth manually was not a common feature of traditional Aboriginal life, but a relatively late development. However, there are earth mounds in western Victoria which, on excavation, have been shown to be the remains of cooking ovens for large animals. These mounds were camped on by the local Aborigines, so once a mound was created it would continue to grow.[40] Whatever the mechanisms were, it is apparent that, at least in western Victoria, direct modification of the landscape, at least on a moderate scale, was in fact taking place during the late Holocene.

Associated with the eel farming complex were structures which came as quite a surprise for the archaeologists who discovered them in 1981— the stone foundations of houses, and in some cases entire villages. Flood gives a good description:

The houses are U-shaped or semi-circular with low stone walls, probably originally about a metre high, with low ceilings of rushes and sheets of bark supported on a timber frame. Most of the houses are only 3 metres in diameter and probably housed just one family.[41]

In one paddock near Lake Condah, 146 of these structures were found. This suggests a population of some 700 people living in a single village.

If the interpretation of the stone circles is correct, this is surely the best example of sedentism amongst Aboriginal people. It is interesting to speculate what the real impact was on the surrounding environment of 700 people living in a confined area, although of course it must be recognised that these structures may not have been occupied simultaneously, and indeed may not be of human construction.[42]

It was not only in the Victorian swamps where such changes are known to have occurred. The presence of complex Aboriginal fish traps on the Barwon River and tidal fish traps on rock platforms in other places around Australia also suggests that the flow of some of the major rivers could have been redirected, at least on a small scale. Piling rows of rocks across a river over a distance of several kilometres also suggests cooperative activity, the kind of activity which could be directed towards landscape modification.

One of the more obvious examples of Aboriginal modification of the environment is the accumulations of shell middens around most of the Australian coastline, virtually all of which are of late Holocene age. Large examples occur in places like Weipa on the west coast of Cape York and on the Clarence River in northern New South Wales. These middens can be anything up to several metres high, and they affect not only the microclimate and microhabitat because of their size, but they also change the pH of the soil. It becomes more alkaline, supporting a different range of plants. Middens also have the effect of stabilising certain areas and acting as sediment traps, particularly if they occur near the mouths of estuaries.

One of the more interesting studies of shell middens was made near the Skew Valley near Dampier on the coast of Western Australia. Two levels were detected, a lower level consisting of *Terebralia*, a mangrove-inhabiting species, and an upper level consisting on the local species of *Anadara*, which occurs at mudbanks exposed at low tide. It has been suggested that 'the change observed from one to the other at Skew Valley is likely to be the result of local environmental change which increased the quantities of the more readily and pleasantly collected bivalves'.[43]

This is one of a number of sites where changes in species composition suggests that changes had been taking place in the sediments of the estuary, with mudflats and mangroves changing their distribution.

Another site at Milingimbi in the Northern Territory also had a greater concentration of whelks (*Terebralia*) and mangrove clams in the lower levels, and *Anadara* near the top. Since these changes were not related to sea-level changes, it is at least possible that they may be related to Aboriginal activity.

Peterson has suggested that once a mound had begun to develop in the tropical north it would become a favoured camping place because it would be drier than the surrounding country, and less heavily infested with mosquitos. Hence it would continue to grow, as it was regularly occupied.[44] Flood suggests that shell mounds were 'excellent living sites: they are dry, good heat insulators, comfortable to sleep on with the aid of a few sheets of bark, and they afford the chance of a sea breeze and a strategic look-out for defensive purposes'.[45]

With the development of localised areas where repeated occupation was likely to lead to a visible physical change in the environment, changes in the species composition of the vegetation was also likely to occur. Certainly for the Anbarra people in Arnhem Land, the practice of breaking the tops off yams and replanting them ensures that the yam beds would continue to flourish, but another practice was even more directed and intentional. The deliberate spitting out of fruit tree seeds into the middens and refuse heaps at the edge of the camps ensured that the fruit trees would be abundant in the areas close to the occupation sites. The middens, rich in decomposing organic material and lime from the shells, provided an ideal medium for the fruit trees to grow in, and ensured that within a few years there would be an abundant supply of fruit in those areas which were already rich in other resources. Indeed, archaeologists in the Northern Territory use the stands of native fruit trees as indicators when they are looking for prehistoric Aboriginal sites. With the growth of fruit trees come other changes in microclimate, so once again the physical landscape will change in addition to the biological landscape.[46]

These impacts were fairly localised, but is it possible to find evidence for changes which were even more widespread? One possible cause of major environmental change is Aboriginal burning. We have already considered the biological consequences, but what about the physical impact?

Researchers as early as the late 1960s like Davies, and later Goede, both of whom worked in Tasmania, suggested that Holocene erosion and valley filling in eastern Tasmania was influenced by Aboriginal burning practices.[47]

In 1981, Hughes and Sullivan published a paper which proposed that fire had been used by Aboriginal hunters and gatherers to the extent that large-scale landscape modification had resulted.[48] Hughes had conducted his doctoral research on the accumulation of deposits in sandstone rock shelters, and had concluded that the deposits in the shelters consisted largely of colluvium — material which had moved down the slope and settled on the floor of the shelter. He noted that the onset of Aboriginal occupation of rock shelters coincided with the onset of sediment accumulation and suggested that 'Aboriginal utilisation of the landscapes in which these sites are set resulted in hillslope instability'.[49] Work undertaken in the sandstone catchments of Mangrove Creek north of Sydney demonstrated that during the late Holocene, there was a marked increase in the erosion of the slopes. They state:

> The hypothesis put forward here is that Aboriginal firing regimes in the dry sclerophyll forested hilly landscapes of eastern Australia led to episodic erosion and deposition at rates which greatly exceeded those under natural firing.[50]

They argue that once regular Aboriginal burning regimes were established, the natural balance was disturbed. The removal of ground cover of grasses and shrubs, and in particular the protective cover of organic litter, exposed the ground surface to accelerated rain splash, sheetwash and rill erosion, especially when burning was followed closely by heavy rain. It is worth noting that the peak rainfall in the Sydney area is primarily in the summer and early autumn, when fires are likely to be common.

That burning does effect erosion had already been clearly demonstrated by many workers. What Hughes and Sullivan were suggesting was that the increased firing frequency resulting from Aboriginal use of the landscape increased local erosion and deposition rates. With accelerated erosion, sediment stripped from the steeper slopes was deposited on the more gentle footslopes or was carried to the valley floors where it either accumulated as valley fills or was washed downstream. This in turn could have resulted in dramatic changes to the aquatic ecosystems, with siltation and its consequent impacts also being blamed on Aboriginal use of fire. It is possible that the changes in shellfish distribution could be related to increased siltation of the estuaries following intensive Aboriginal burning.

Hickin and Page had observed ten years earlier that there was a dramatic increase in valley filling in the drainage basins of Mangrove Creek, Wollombi Brook and the MacDonald and Colo Rivers. They dated this sedimentation at between 4000 and 1500 years ago.[51] Blong found that several metres of alluvium had accumulated in the MacDonald River within the last 1800 years.[52] Others workers have reported similar phenomena in the Illawarra district and on the New South Wales north coast. The late Holocene age of these fills eliminates the possibility that they were associated with changes in sea level, which have been relatively stable for the last 6000 years, so it is hard to imagine any cause other than human impact.

The reason why there should have been a dramatic increase in firing frequency was also suggested by Hughes and Sullivan — intensification of land-use practices reflecting late-Holocene population increase. Other workers had observed that the high levels of charcoal in the upper levels of Lake George may have been related to increased Aboriginal burning in the catchment.[53] Singh, Kershaw and Clark all observed that the fire-sensitive and moisture-demanding plant species only disappeared during the Holocene, and this is apparent at a number of sites with good pollen sequences. Kershaw resorted to the claim that the swamp surface was burning in order to explain dramatic increases in charcoal during the mid-Holocene at Lynch's Crater.[54]

Clearly there were some areas which were likely to be impacted by Aboriginal burning. The sandstone areas, or other soils with low clay content, tend to erode rapidly if heavy rain follows a fire. Some areas will not burn. Rainforests are unlikely to burn because of the high moisture content. Interestingly, Lampert and Sanders document changes in the relative distribution of rainforest remnants and sclerophyll vegetation on the Beecroft Peninsular at Jervis Bay, and suggest that regular Aboriginal burning may have had some impact at least on the margins of the rainforests.[55]

There is a growing body of evidence which suggests that Aboriginal land practices during the late Holocene were increasingly having an impact on the physical environment. Whether it was accumulation of shell mounds in Arnhem Land, building canals and traps in western Victoria, causing sedimentation in the valley floors and siltation of the rivers due to increased burning along the east coast, or simply enlarging rock holes so that they would hold more water in the arid zone, the increasing Aboriginal population was certainly having a much more direct effect on the environment than their Pleistocene ancestors. One of the results of an increasing population is that there is likely to be greater competition for resources, which may also cause impacts on the environment.

If we accept that Aboriginal populations grew significantly during the late Holocene, either as a result of the introduction of new technologies or because of more efficient use of resources, then we must also accept that as the population increased, some resources may have become more difficult to acquire. These resources may have been as basic as food, or as insignificant as the right kind of bird feathers for decoration. However, it seems likely that accompanying the growing populations, there was a growing competition between Aboriginal groups for those resources. This competition may have impacted on both the physical and the social environment.

Not all the evidence for change in resource utilisation is clear-cut. It seems apparent that within the last few thousand years some old resources became increasingly replaced by new ones — kangaroos and wallabies were not hunted to the same extent, or at least they were hunted in a different way requiring a cooperation between groups. Such levels of interaction and cooperation were necessary to build fish traps, canals, stone houses and some of the other large constructions. The suggestion that social interaction increased in the recent past seems apparent from these data, but it is also interesting to note that this social interaction extended to sharing resources which became available within the territory of one group with people from other areas — indeed, with people who spoke different languages.

There are several account of whales being beached in the Sydney region in the 1790s and early 1800s. When this happened, Aborigines travelled from distances of up to 200 km to share in the whale feast. Certainly people travelled from Newcastle and Nowra to eat a whale which was beached at Sydney, and Sydney people travelled to Newcastle to share in a whale which was beached there.[56]

Similar interactions were apparent when it came to seasonally abundant resources. In the Southern Highlands, bogong moths migrate in their millions from their breeding grounds to the alps between November and February, and there they congregate in caves and in crevasses, covering the walls like a carpet. Flood suggests that the density can get as high as 14,000 per square metre.[57] They have abdomens which are full of fat, and they were roasted for about two minutes on a fire and eaten. This rich diet is reported to have made the Aborigines 'sleek and fat after several weeks or even months feasting on moths'.[58]

The moths provided a focus of both economic and social activity. The main groups gathered at places like Jindabyne and initiation ceremonies, marriages and the settling of disputes were all part of the activities before the ascent to the mountains to gorge on moths. At one site in the highlands, Bogong Cave contained a mortar and pestle for grinding up the moths, and charcoal from the same layer gave a date of around 1000 years ago.[59] Flood, who studied this area for her doctoral thesis, argues that there was very little use of these mountain areas until the advent of the small tool tradition — that is, only within the last 4000 years, and that it was only seasonal summer occupation then. She argues that moth hunters could have probably exploited the moths in their own territory, but instead they travelled distances of more than 100 km to concentrate in the upper mountains — suggesting that the social activity was at least as important as the economic one. Interestingly, apparently only the men hunted the moths in the upper mountains, while the women and children camped in the valleys, almost certainly so the men could carry out ceremonial activities.

The practice of travelling long distances to share resources continued after the arrival of Europeans in Australia. When Governor Macquarie decided to establish an annual feast for Aborigines at Parramatta in 1814, people travelled from enormous distances to be present at the gathering. In 1824, Aborigines from as far away as Bathurst and Port Macquarie attended.[60] Clearly this concept of different tribes coming together to exploit an abundant resource was well accepted, even if the resource was being provided by Europeans.

Why was it accepted that tribes would travel great distances to participate in events like bogong moth exploitation in the Southern Highlands, bunya nut exploitation in southern Queensland, whale beachings all along the coastline, burrawang feasts and kangaroo hunts? How was this related to other social interactions?

To answer these questions we must first try to understand how long these processes took place, and indeed what factor or factors resulted in Aboriginal people developing greater levels of social interaction. Has Aboriginal culture always been essentially the same, with groups from different geographic regions sharing their food resources while maintaining traditional rights of access? Surely this process could not have arisen because of increasing competition for resources — or could it?

The indicators of increasing human population suggested by Cohen were proposed for agricultural and herding communities, and not for Aboriginal culture.[61] However, there are some strong parallels. Taking care to avoid circular arguments, the indicators do suggest an Aboriginal population increase. Lourandos followed on from Cohen's suggestions by pointing out that there were several other archaeological indicators of intensification — which he maintained was associated with population increase.[62]

Lourandos suggested that intensification, associated with population increase and greater social interaction, could be identified by

- increase in intensity of site usage;

- increased rate of establishment of new sites;

- increased usage of marginal environments;

- increased complexity of site economy; or

- increased complexity of exchange systems.

One of the indicators is movement into marginal areas, and exploiting low-level resources. It is of interest, then, to consider Aboriginal settlement in the arid zone, which was certainly well developed at the time Europeans arrived in Australia.

There was a general abandonment of sites in the arid zone between peak glaciation until around 4000 years ago. Veth has argued that the arid zone consisted of barriers, corridors and refuges for human populations. He believes the sandy deserts have always been barriers, and that as the glacial climate further dried out the arid zone the corridors were also abandoned, with occupation concentrated in those areas which had enough water to support Aboriginal populations.[63]

However, it is clear that as the climate warmed during the late Pleistocene and early Holocene, the pattern of Aboriginal settlement changed — associated with the advent of new technologies and social networks — and many sites were occupied for the first time within the last 4000 years.

Although sites on the Nullarbor Plain near the coast were occupied perhaps as early as 8000 years ago, occupation was sparse until 4000 years ago, when the density of both food remains and stone artefacts increased dramatically. At Allens Cave there was a dramatic increase in artefact discard rates and the intensity of site usage.[64] At Hawker Lagoon there was virtually no evidence of occupation between 15,000 and 5000 years ago, at a time when the water level in the lagoon was at its greatest. Lampert and Hughes argue that:

> A moister climate allowed people to spread more widely across the landscape, occupying on a more regular basis areas that later became inhospitable as aridity and salinity increased. Under these conditions there was less need for people to fall back on to the major water sources that later became popular.[65]

Some time after 5000 years ago, Hawker Lagoon became much more intensively occupied, with large numbers of stone tools, fireplaces and seed grinders.

At Walga Rock in the Murchison Basin of Western Australia, there is evidence of sparse occupation between 9000 and 7000 years ago, then a hiatus followed by and then reoccupation around 3000 years ago.[66] All other arid zone sites, especially those in the sandy deserts, are mid to late Holocene in age, with most of them less than 1000 years old. Mound Springs sites are all less than 5000 years old. Smith has excavated fifteen sites in Central Australia, all of which were first occupied between 3500 and 3000 years ago. At all these sites, there is a dramatic increase in the range and quantity of debris in the last 850 years, with a much greater range of raw materials being used.[67]

Sites on Coopers Creek, the edge of the Simpson Desert, Coongie Lakes and the Victorian Mallee all show the same pattern. The arid zone was sparsely occupied during the Pleistocene and early Holocene, with an increase in site usage around 4000 years ago followed by an even greater intensity of site usage in the last 1000 years.[68]

Although Smith has suggested that environmental change may well have been the stimulus for the changes in the arid zone, there is little evidence to support this. The arid zone has essentially been arid since the late Pleistocene, and the Holocene is relatively stable period. If this is so, then why and how is there a more intense use of sites relatively recently? Clearly the logical reason is increasing populations leading to marginal areas like the arid zone being used. While it is possible to explain the intensification between 4000 and 3000 years ago as being linked to the technological changes associated with the advent of the small tool tradition, the same cannot be said for the changes which have occurred in the last 1000 years.

Veth perhaps best sums up the situation: 'a combination of demographic pressure, technological shifts and changes in social structure would have enabled the colonisation and permanent occupation of the marginal sandy deserts from approximately 5000 BP'.[69]

Veth touches on the third aspect of occupation of the marginal areas — changes in social structure. What is being argued is that increasing population has led not only to occupation of marginal environments but also to changes in the social organisation to enable these environments to be successfully exploited.[70]

We may be seeing the same phenomenon of greater social interaction in the arid zone as has been observed in southeastern Australia with cooperative kangaroo hunting, bogong moth exploitation and travelling great distances to exploit beached whales. In order to exploit the Australian environment, Aboriginal social structure changed. In order to adapt to a new range of environments, under conditions of high population density, social and cultural changes were required.

In the arid zone, it is possible to see why and how this increased social interaction and networking became established. As populations increased and regular water became a problem, in order to cope with the possibility of drought or other severe limitation of resources, mechanisms had to be established so that if a particular group was placed under stress, they had a way out — that is, they had the opportunity to avail themselves of the resources of neighbours who were better off than themselves. In turn, if their neighbours found themselves in difficulty because of lack of water or food, the neighbours would be entitled to utilise the resources of the adjoining groups.

Such increases in reliance on your neighbour would certainly necessitate greater social interaction to maintain these bonds. Perhaps the social structure which consequently developed extended into other areas — trading networks, wife exchange between tribes, and sharing ceremonies. One of the things which is apparent in the arid zone within the last 1000 years is the dramatic increase in the range of raw materials which were being used for the manufacture of stone tools. Stone was apparently being traded over large distances. We can begin to see how the developing networks and social interactions may have impacted on the environment. Aboriginal groups needed to exploit more of their local resources than were enough for their own use — they had to provide materials for trade and exchange — to provide an abundance of food for certain ceremonies, essentially to increase the productivity of the land, not only to support their own population but to facilitate exchange and trade with adjacent groups.

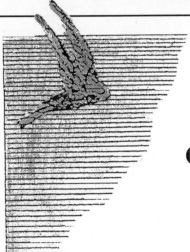

CHAPTER 8

The impact
of European
settlement

During the time that Aboriginal people have occupied the Australian continent, the vegetation composition has changed in response to changing climate. Only during the last few thousand years a relatively stable climate, together with Aboriginal burning practices, has resulted in the development of the vegetation patterns which were evident when Europeans arrived in 1788.

Throughout the late Holocene, Aborigines exploited their environment successfully, using a wide range of plants and animals for food. The number of food plants used was enormous. Literally hundreds of different fruits, roots, shoots, tubers, flowers and leaves were eaten. It was the intimate knowledge of where and when each of these resources would be available which enabled Aborigines to successfully exploit their territories.

Some resources provided dietary staples. Across Australia, a variety of plants with underground tubers rich in starch were exploited. These plants are colloquially referred to as 'yams', and although they include true yams they also include a diverse range of plants from many different families. The exploitation of the yam beds was an essential component of the economic strategy of Aboriginal people in many areas. Hallam, referring to yam beds in Western Australia, states that: 'Gathering yams was anything but a random process... it was certainly not a matter of digging out a root here and there, but of returning regularly to extensively used tracts'.[1]

Once European settlement began in the Sydney area, the impact on the flora and fauna was almost immediate. Clearing of the land resulted in the loss of habitat for a wide range of animals, and they became locally rare. The large animals, the kangaroos, wallabies and emus, were the first to be affected. Some of these animals were hunted by Europeans to supplement their own meagre food reserves.

The coastal Aboriginal people depended heavily on fish and shellfish, while the people who lived west of Parramatta, more than 30 km from the coast, relied on a much wider range of foods.[2] It was these inland clans who suffered most when farms were established along the Hawkesbury River and their yam beds were destroyed. By June 1795, the vast majority of the yam beds had been replaced with crops. When the Aborigines attempted to harvest the crops which grew on the river banks, they were driven off. A few settlers maintained good relations with the Aborigines, but others shot any Aborigine they saw on their land. The two economic systems were competing for the same rich soil to provide food, a circumstance which inevitably led to conflict.[3]

The Rev. Fyshe Palmer, writing in June 1795 to Doctor John Disney in London, confirms that it was the loss of the yam beds which caused the conflict: 'The natives of the Hawkesbury lived on the wild yams on the banks. Cultivation has rooted out these, and poverty compelled them to steal Indian corn to support nature. The unfeeling settlers resented this by unparalleled severities'.[4]

One of the methods the Aborigines used to obtain food was to burn the underbrush. These techniques were incompatible with European farming methods, and many reported 'attacks' on farms were probably a result of Aborigines burning the landscape as it was their custom to do.

Once Aboriginal populations were driven away from settled areas, and when traditional burning patterns ceased, there were clearly visible changes in the vegetation associations.

The extent to which anthropogenic fire was available as a source of ignition at least since European settlement is clearly reflected in most ethnographic accounts. Quotes like the following are common throughout the literature: 'Every individual of the tribe when travelling to or going a distance from their encampment, carries a fire-stick for the purpose of kindling fires'.[5]

In Western Australia, the ethnographic accounts suggest that fires were used by the men to clear the landscape to make travel easier. Hallam suggests that 'firing was both a deliberate part of such usage and an accidental consequence'.[6] However, other recent ethnographic accounts in Arnhem Land support the view that there

was very little accidental about it. Pyne describes the burning practices of the Gunei tribe, and reports that burning actually starts at
'special sites while the rainy season is still in progress. It escalates
as drying spreads... and it culminates at the end of the Dry with a
conflagration of those places destined for burning but not yet fired'.[7]
He clearly suggests that there is controlled, planned, directed burning
taking place.

The reasons for the different stages of burning are also proposed,
although Aboriginal informants would not necessarily concur with the
suggested reasons why they traditionally burn in a particular fashion
or in a particular sequence. Pyne argues that protective early burning
acts like a firebreak to prevent damage to the rainforests. The burning
regime of different habitats is varied, and 'lowland sites tend to burn
annually; upland sites on a cycle of two, three or even four years. In a
landscape in which several fire regimes are imaginable, Aborigines
imposed one that suited their purposes'.[8]

Such burning practices may result in both increases and
decreases of some animal species in the short term. Waterfowl thrive
in sedges which regenerate shortly after burning, but snakes have
nowhere to hide and disappear into the surrounding bush.

To counter the claim that many of the results of Aboriginal
burning are accidental, there are many accounts in the literature
which demonstrate conclusively that Aboriginal people were using
fire in a well-planned manner. Pyne suggests that the people in
Arnhem Land

> exercise control by timing the fires with diurnal wind shifts, by relying
> on the evening humidity, and by exploiting topographic features like
> cliffs and streams and old burns. The fires were sequential, and burning
> a composite of practices in a mosaic of environments that extended over
> nine to ten months. Most of the grasslands and savannahs burned; por-
> tions of the floodplains burned twice; the woodlands and forests burned
> on the order of a fourth to a half their area.[9]

Implicit in this statement is the view that some areas are intentionally burned and some are left unburned — mosaic burning. Pyne
goes on to suggest that

> What distinguished the Aboriginal regime was the amount of burning
> that occurred in the midseason, the regularity of the annual burning
> cycle, the biological timing of the fires, the insistence that some areas
> never be fired and that others be fired as often as possible.[10]

There can be little doubt that this burning pattern in Arnhem
Land favoured some species at the expense of others. It is unlikely

that *Callitris* could have survived a pattern of late-season burns, or that woodlands could have endured a 'relentless late burning on an annual basis', or that rainforest enclaves could have thrived without the protective early burning. The fire regime in Arnhem Land is one of regular burning; sequential burning; variable burning; and mosaic burning.[11] In many ways, it is the strong seasonality in the tropical north which determines when fires will be lit. In other parts of Australia, where rainfall is not divided into a consistent wet and dry season, other patterns were developed.

In the desert areas, several factors may influence burning patterns. Rainfall, or lack of it, is sporadic and unpredictable, and can override any man-made firing regime. If there is no standing crop then there is nothing to burn, so there are no fires. If the land is underwater, there are no fires. Unlike Arnhem Land, there is no defined wet and dry season on which the burning pattern can be based. Under these circumstances, when conditions did allow an area to burn, the fire could burn over much wider distances. It is possible to view Central Australia as an area where Aboriginal burning of particularly valuable areas may indeed have protected these areas from more intense wildfires which could otherwise have been initiated by lightning strikes.

The impact of the cessation of Aboriginal burning in the arid zone became clear in the 1920s and 1930s, when traditional people began to move from the deserts into the missions and reserves. Without regular burning, large wildfires broke out in the 1920s, 1950s and again in the 1970s, initiated by lightning strikes.[12] Because there was such an accumulation of fuel, due to the cessation of regular burning, when fire did break out it was unusually large and it resulted in large-scale localised extinction of the medium-sized animals — those with body weights between 45 grams and 5 kg. In those places where traditional burning regimes remained — for example, the Pintubi tribal lands in the Gibson desert — the medium-sized animals survived.[13] Clearly there was an association between the fire regime and the survival of the small to medium sized mammals. Admittedly, by the 1920s other changes had occurred in Central Australia — exotic plants and animals had become established, and Europeans had begun to impact on the margins of the deserts with their land-management practices.

In 1974 and 1975, 80% of Uluru National Park was burnt by a fire, an event which simply could not have happened if traditional Aboriginal burning practices had continued. Now, these traditional burning practices are being incorporated into the parks plan of management.[14]

At the other end of the continent in Tasmania, there are some clear examples of Aboriginal burning maintaining particular environments at the expense of others. When burning stopped in the early nineteenth century, grasslands degenerated into scrub, eucalypt forest became wet sclerophyll forest and eventually rainforest. Along the west coast, a narrow band of heath and sedge gave way to encroaching rainforest. Lieutenant Henry Bunbury explained that

> we could never do it [burn] with the same judgement and good effect as the natives, who keep the fire within due bounds, only burning those parts they wish when the scrub becomes too thick or when they have another object to gain by it.[15]

We have exactly the same effects happening on Kangaroo Island around 2500 years ago. Grasslands became woodlands and scrub, Casuarina increased dramatically, and charcoal levels in Lashmar's Lagoon also increased significantly, suggesting infrequent high-intensity burns had replaced frequent low-intensity burns. These changes correspond to the time when Aboriginal people abandoned or died out on Kangaroo Island.[16]

The impact of changing fire regimes is not as simple as these examples may suggest. Once the fire regime changes, both the plants and animals will respond in different ways. On Rottnest Island there were no eucalypts and the vegetation simply did not burn. There was no Aboriginal population, and the vegetation was dominated by acacias, cypress pine and Melaleuca. When Europeans settled Rottnest Island, they cleared and burned the landscape. In 1956, wildfires swept the island and the acacias and melaleucas failed to regenerate. In this case, the European use of fire had not resulted in the kinds of vegetation associations which had evolved under Aboriginal burning regimes on the mainland. The European burning had resulted in a dramatic increase in the population of quokkas, small rabbit-sized macropods. The quokkas grazed on the seed-regenerated scleromorphs and promoted tussock grass, which were better suited to both fires and quokkas. In this case, human intervention resulted in an increase in the quokka population which resulted in changes in the vegetation which resulted, following an intense fire, in virtual extinction of many plant species.[17]

The general interrelationship between plants, animals, Aborigines and fire has been clearly established. But what is the impact on the specific vegetation associations and animal species? Crucial to understanding the changes is an appreciation of the concept of vegetation succession.

Noble and Slatyer describe the classical view of succession in the following terms: 'following a disturbance, several assemblages of species progressively occupy a site, each giving way to its successor until a community finally develops which is able to reproduce itself indefinitely'.[18]

This final community is often described as a climax community, and it is implied that the climax community is in equilibrium with the prevailing environment. Noble and Slatyer argue that the composition of a community which is exposed to fire is dependent on 'the availability of particular species at the particular site and their ability to become established and grow at that site',[19] and further that 'the significance of a particular fire as a source of disturbance depends... on the normal pattern of fire frequency and intensity which prevails in the community and at a site under consideration'.[20]

If fire is rare in a community, then a fire may result in the loss of species, but where fire is common, and where most species are fire-adapted, most species will have effective strategies for survival and will therefore not be adversely impacted in the long term, although of course there may be short term reductions in the number of individuals within the community. However, even in communities which are adapted to fire, adaption is to a particular fire frequency–intensity regime. A change in the regime can also result in a reduction in the number of species. A good example is a plant which is killed by fire and which produces short-lived seed. Successive fires can eliminate these species from a community. This is the kind of problem which managers of National Parks are trying to cope with at the moment. If they do not burn the parks, some species will become extinct. If they do burn the park, other species may become extinct.

Where does this leave communities which are adapted to regular low-intensity burns initiated by Aboriginal people? Noble and Slatyer suggest that in fire-adapted communities, succession 'has virtually no applicability, even when the fire frequency is strongly aperiodic and perhaps associated with a particular management strategy'.[21] The communities which develop under these fire regimes are self-sustaining. Succession will only be important if the fire regime changes. The mosaic burning patterns used by Aboriginal people resulted in the formation of a mosaic of communities which will remain stable in the long term, provided the same firing pattern continues.

The changes which have been observed following the cessation of Aboriginal burning are therefore successional ones induced by a changed fire regime, specifically the reduction in fire frequency. The generalised successional sequence might go something like this: grass or sedge > shrub > scrub > sclerophyll forest > mixed forest > rainforest. This sequence will of course be influenced by other factors, such as rainfall and soil type.

When the fire frequency is reduced, then there is a greater likeli-hood that the next stage in the sequence will be reached. Conversely, under normal circumstances, without anthropogenic fires, rainforest will burn less than mixed forest which will burn less than sclerophyll forest.

Impact of Aboriginal burning on fauna

For the Australian fauna, there are literally hundreds of studies which document the responses of birds and animals to fire. Populations of most species survive even intense fires. All species return to the forest as soon as it reaches the stage of growth which will support them, generally within five years. Some species are mobile and can escape from a fire, to recolonise later. Others burrow under the ground, some take refuge in unburnt areas, and others shelter under rocks. However, in extreme fires, such as the one which occurred in Nadgee Nature Reserve on the New South Wales south coast in 1972, large numbers of birds, kangaroos, possums and other large mammals were killed.[22]

Large mammals generally survive fires because of their mobility. In one study of 26 bettongs and 4 tammar wallabies, only one bettong died in a fire, while the others survived by either sheltering or dou-bling back through the fire onto burnt ground.[23]

There is always a decline in abundance immediately following fires, due to lack of food and increased visibility and chance of preda-tion. The initial decrease in wallabies and kangaroos at Nadgee after the 1972 fire was caused by an increase in dingo predation.[24]

Repopulation after fire does not represent a classical mammalian succession. Early post-fire vegetation will suit some species like the house mouse, but gradually other species like the rats and marsupial mice will return. In the case of macropods and wallabies, one study by Christensen and Kimber in Western Australia showed that grey kangaroos and brush wallabies showed an annual decline in number over five years following a fire.[25] The post-fire succession is therefore complex, and indeed varying frequency of firing can impact different-ly on different species. Birds and reptiles have been shown to respond in the same way as the mammals, with the complexity of the vegetation associations being closely correlated with the diversity of bird species.[26]

One of the more interesting indicators of post-fire succession is the availability of nitrogen in the ecosystem. Leguminous nodule-pro-ducing native plants regenerate the nitrogen lost following fire, and this in turn has been shown to be closely correlated to the success of many of the macropods. In the absence of fires, the legumes age and die. The carrying capacity in respect to wallabies of both the arid zone and the southwest forests in Western Australia has been shown to be linked to the availability of nitrogen. It seems that the replenished nitrogen levels after fire allows the grasses to grow, favouring the wallabies which feed on them. Without fires, the legumes disappear, the grasses disappear, the wallabies disappear and are replaced by kangaroos.[27]

The strong interrelationship between plants, animals and fire is apparent in Australia. Such relationships evolved because the Australian vegetation was exposed to fire long before Aborigines arrived on the continent.

Plants and animals in dry sclerophyll communities coexist in dynamic equilibrium because the structure, size and distribution of populations is constantly changing. The creation of vegetation mosaics based on frequency of firing by Aboriginal people therefore must be seen as a mechanism for increasing the range of habitats, the range of stages of regeneration after burning, and therefore the range of microenvironments. In terms of the overall species diversity, such a pattern would increase the total number of species because it maximises the habitat range. Some species will be disadvantaged and the populations will decline; others will be advantaged but the overall biodiversity will be maintained.

At least over the last few thousand years, regular low-intensity mosaic burning has provided the opportunity for all of the plant and animal species to find a niche somewhere, and the burning patterns have not shifted the evolutionary trends within Australia. What has caused such changes is the restriction of habitat variability and the contraction of habitat area which followed European settlement.

Impact of Aborigines on other carnivores

Aboriginal people are predators — they have hunted a wide range of animals, perhaps megafauna during the Pleistocene, but certainly macropods, possums, rats, bats, fish, birds and reptiles. Has the level of predation of Aborigines impacted on other carnivores? We have already discussed the relationship between the dingo and Aborigines, but what about the relationships with marsupial carnivores?

Before about 5000 years ago, there were two or possibly three carnivores larger than cat size. These were the thylacine, or Tasmanian tiger, the *Sarcophilus*, or Tasmanian devil, and the Pleistocene marsupial lion, *Thylacoleo*, which was probably extinct by 20,000 years ago and possibly much earlier. It is convenient to lump the extinction of *Thylacoleo* with the other megafaunal extinctions, and suggest that climate change had a significant if not total part to play in its demise. However, it is only within the last few thousand years that there have been dramatic reductions and mainland extinctions of the thylacine and devil. It is very easy to assume that these two animals became extinct through competition from the dingo following its arrival after 5000 years ago, but there are other possibilities. Did the thylacine become extinct because of competition with the dingo or a combination of competition with the dingo, competition with an ever-increasing Aboriginal population, and environmental change induced by Aboriginal burning? All three factors seem to have occurred at about the same time, yet the impact of direct competition from Aborigines through overhunting or the impact of more intense burning have not been seriously considered.

It is wise to take note of some comments of Eric Guiler, whose book, *Thylacine: The Tragedy of the Tasmanian Tiger*, documents many accounts of thylacine behaviour and ecology. It is relevant to note that: 'Thylacines did not occur in large numbers in Tasmania during the early colonial era and subsequently it always was a matter for record or comment when one was seen or trapped'.[28] That thylacines were not common in Tasmania was confirmed by the fact that 'Jeffreys (1820) stated that only four [thylacines] had been seen since settlement [in 1803]'.[29]

The fact that the two large marsupial carnivores survived in Tasmania strongly suggests that factors other then climate were responsible for their extinctions on the mainland. Guiler believed that the thylacines and devils were outcompeted by the dingo. He states 'Dogs would compete with thylacines for food but would have a distinct ecological advantage as thylacines do not eat carrion or vegetation and are not known to use any form of pack hunting'.[30]

The possibility that the thylacines could have been driven to extinction by Aboriginal hunting was dismissed by Guiler: 'The continental thylacines may well have suffered predation by Aborigines but it is unlikely that this would be a major cause of their extinction'.[31] He argues that the thylacine population in Tasmania was relatively low until the 1870s, when it increased. Between 1884 and 1910 between 100 and 300 thylacines a year were killed for their bounty. A total of 2110 bounties were paid between 1888 and 1909. Guiler argues that disease between 1905 and 1910, which also impacted on devils, tiger cats and native cats, was the main factor which led to their extinction.[32]

Guiler also notes that by the 1850s there were large numbers of wild dogs in Tasmania, and that these were killing far more sheep than the thylacines. Dogs were, in general, afraid of thylacines, which were reported to have killed and eaten them.

There is an interesting pattern in Tasmania — low thylacine population density without dogs but with Aborigines, followed by high population densities with dogs but without Aborigines. It could be argued that the increase in sheep populations caused the increase in thylacine numbers, but in fact the sheep populations fell in Tasmania between the early 1870s and the late 1880s. And what of the other carnivore, the Tasmanian devil? Their population density is still high. They survive competition with wild dogs, probably because they are scavengers.

There are no simple answers to these apparently contradictory observations. I would summarise by saying that if it wasn't competition from dingoes that caused the thylacine to become extinct on the mainland, and it wasn't Aboriginal burning, which seems unlikely because burning would have increased the number of prey animals and increased the area of the thylacines preferred environment, could it have been Aboriginal overhunting or competition for prey? Certainly this is a possibility worth considering.

The most likely scenario is that the combination of dingoes, new hunting technologies and increased Aboriginal population density resulted in extreme pressure on mainland thylacine populations, ultimately driving them to extinction. In Tasmania, Aboriginal burning still occurred and the thylacine population seemed to increase, even after wild dogs were introduced in the nineteenth century, so Aboriginal hunting or competition probably played an important role in controlling numbers. It may have been the effective removal of a predator, the traditional Tasmanian Aborigines, which enabled the thylacine population to increase during the mid to late nineteenth century.

Aboriginal impact on large herbivores

At high Aboriginal population densities, the harvesting rates of kangaroos were low, and kangaroo populations were also kept low. These impacts are dependent on high Aboriginal population densities, which only seem to be a phenomenon associated with the last few thousand years. Prior to around 5000 years ago, the Aboriginal population would have largely followed the general availability of resources. Perhaps a simple predator–prey relationship existed between Aborigines and macropods; if the availability of macropods decreased it is more likely that Aborigines exploited other resources. This option was open to them, provided their population density was low.

One possible model of recent Aboriginal impact suggests that as the population increased, and the population of kangaroos declined under increased hunting pressure, measures were introduced to increase the number of macropods. Burning the landscape increased macropod habitat and therefore increased the number of macropods which could be hunted. As the Aboriginal population continued to grow, fewer and fewer macropods were consumed and other sources of protein were exploited. More birds, reptiles, fish, eels, crayfish, shellfish, possums and bandicoots were incorporated into the diet.[33]

We have seen that other late technological developments like eel farming, fish traps, shell fishhooks, and probably the greater use of canoes, all contributed to the capacity for a larger population to be supported.

So could this series of technological changes be sustained? Or would the growing pressure on resources due to the increased Aboriginal population have resulted in further changes to the population level of animals and additional modification to the vegetation and the environment? Indeed, can the fact that seeds were being traded and sown in Central Australia, the fact that yams were being replanted all over the country, the fact that fruit seeds were spread around regular camp sites, and the fact that stone huts were built in western Victoria, be seen as phases of a trend which indicates where Aboriginal culture was already heading — towards agriculture, animal domestication and permanent settlements. If so, we must seriously ask ourselves: was Aboriginal use of resources in fact sustainable development, or do the changes in resource base which seem to occur over the recent period of Aboriginal occupation of Australia really tell us that traditional Aboriginal culture, as it existed in 1788 and much later in some parts of Australia, could not have been sustained indefinitely?

CHAPTER 9

Contemporary Aboriginal societies

Since the arrival of Europeans in Australia, Aboriginal people have been dispossessed from their traditional lands, and their culture forced to adapt to at least some aspects of the European lifestyle. However, in many parts of Australia, notably Arnhem Land, Central Australia, the Kimberleys, Cape York and the Western Desert, Aboriginal people have retained control over large areas of land. The conservation value of land which is controlled by Aboriginal people is well recognised by conservationists and politicians alike. There are also implications for Aboriginal management of land arising out of the Native Title decision, and it seems highly likely that additional tracts of land will be handed back to traditional Aboriginal owners.[1]

In many cases, the traditional Aboriginal owners still use their land to obtain food. However, they have adopted many modern conveniences in order to improve the effectiveness of their hunting and gathering, and they often mix European goods and traditional foods. It is useful to examine the practices of some of these Aboriginal communities and see how contemporary Aboriginal societies impact on their landscape.

Several important studies have been carried out in a range of environments, and these provide a broad perspective on present impacts on land which, in some cases, has been subjected to European land-use practices for more than 100 years.

Typical of many Aboriginal outstations in Arnhem Land is

Momega outstation, about 100 km east of the Alligator Rivers region. Research was conducted there by John Altman, who saw two factors as being particularly important in tropical Australia — the potential Aboriginal bioresources which could be exploited by Europeans, and the way Aboriginal people used the land, bearing in mind that Europeans have continually failed to successfully develop the tropical north.[2]

Altman conducted anthropological fieldwork among the eastern Gunwinggu in the Mann–Liverpool Rivers region. He confirms that what he records is 'modern' rather than 'traditional' Aboriginal use of bush foods. He worked over 296 days during one entire seasonal cycle. The only comparative detailed study was that of Betty Meehan amongst the Anbarra people.[3]

Momega is a semi-permanent camp which is used as a base by the eastern Gunwinggu. The people lived a semi-nomadic lifestyle and often camped away from Momega for long periods of time, generally depending on the availability of game in other areas and for attendance at ceremonies. The size of the group varied from 18 to 44 people and averaged 31 over the season. The range used by this band was about 600 square km, but it was shared by other Gunwinggu bands based at other locations. Momega is therefore typical of about 25 other outstations in the Maningrida area of Arnhem Land.

As is the case with most of the Arnhem Land area, there is a strong seasonality to the climate, with the wet season extending from October to March and the dry from May to September. As in precontact times, the seasonal factor today is a key determinant of camp location and the degree of mobility. The main factor which influences the location of the band is the availability of subsistence resources at different locations, or 'resource bases'. 'Today, however, seasonal movements are not as well defined as in the past for two reasons: access to modern transport and market foodstuffs'.[4]

In general, to use a 'resource base' a band must live close to it. Motor vehicles can greatly extend a group's access to bush foods. During his work at Momega, Altman reported that the Gunwinggu used vehicles only on 31 days, or about 10% of the time. He noted that the availability of 'market foods' meant that large ceremonial gatherings could be held 'at seasonally uncharacteristic times'.[5]

Regardless of the shop-bought foods and motor vehicles, there are definite seasonal movements to exploit resources. During the early and late wet season the band is relatively sedentary, but by late March or April the band adopts a semi-nomadic lifestyle. The initial move is about 10–12 km towards the tidal reaches of the Liverpool River, where fish are readily available. By late April or early May the second movement begins — east 11 km to the Mimanyar region to exploit bird life and fish and later 8 km north to Bulgai for the annual fish harvest on the Tomkinson flood plains.[6]

By August, the fresh-water supplies start to disappear and the band disperses into smaller family groups which spread throughout the range. During the late dry season the main regional ceremonies begin and the band reunites and converges on the ceremonial locations. Following these ceremonies, the band returns to the wet season camp at Momega.[7]

During the course of the year, the Gunwinggu were observed eating 90 animal species and 80 plant species. The Gunwinggu reported at least another 20 plant foods which they also traditionally use. Altman estimated that 47% of the kilocalories and 81% of the protein in the diet of the Momega people came from bush foods. He also noted that although 80 plant species were eaten, their overall contribution to the diet was insignificant, with the maximum monthly floral contribution only 8%. In contrast, fauna contributed over 90% of the bush food's diet each month. The most difficult times, both traditionally and today, are the wet seasons, when the contribution of bush foods declines, probably because much of the land is under water. The low use of plant foods is almost certainly related to the availability of flour and sugar, which are both cheap and readily available. In contrast, 'the digging of bush carbohydrates like yams, lily pods, spike rush corms, etc, is extremely labour intensive and is the least efficient production process in the subsistence economy'.[8]

> The significance of hunting and fishing activities, undertaken primarily by men, has increased. This is due to two factors. First, introduced technology (particularly shotguns, but also fishing lures, fish wires, etc.) has not only been readily adapted to traditional production processes, but has increased their efficiency. Second, introduced feral game, like water buffalo, cattle and pig, are used and during some months account for 20% of bush food returns.[9]

In summary, the people who use the Momega outstation continue to hunt and gather on their land, and continue to follow the traditional patterns. Kangaroos are still hunted by firing the landscape late in the dry season, but water buffalo, wild cattle and pigs now also form an important component of the diet. The use of vehicles extends the range of travel, and therefore the ease with which particular foods can be obtained, while shotguns and fish lures make hunting more efficient. On the other hand, the plant-gathering and processing of the women has been drastically reduced, largely because of the availability of store-bought flour and sugar. What we are seeing is a shift not only in the diet, but also in the varying contributions of men and women to the diet.

At Momega, the impact of the Aboriginal people on their environment is not significantly different from what it was prior to European settlement, except that hunting has become more important and easier. What impact these shifts in resource base will have on the terrestrial animal populations remains to be determined.

A second approach of contemporary Aboriginal communities is that adopted by the Mowanjum people who live near Derby in the Kimberley Region of Western Australia. Part of their time is spent in Derby and part of it on their cattle station and traditional lands at Pantijan, one and a half days travel by four wheel drive vehicle from Derby. O'Dea and colleagues carried out a nutritional study on a group of people while they were in Derby and then for seven weeks when they 'went bush'.[10] They reported on the different diets.

Urban diet: flour, sugar, rice, carbonated drinks, alcoholic beverages (beer and port), powdered milk, cheap fatty meats, potatoes, onions and variable contributions of other fresh fruit and vegetables. (50% carbohydrate, 40% fat, 10% protein.)

Bush diet (inland): meat (beef, kangaroo, crocodiles, birds), freshwater fish, turtle, shellfish, yams, figs, honey. (10% carbohydrate, 40% fat, 50% protein.)

Bush diet (coast): seafood, birds, kangaroo (lack of vegetable foods). (< 5% carbohydrate, 20% fat, 80% protein.)[11]

It can be seen that the ability to travel using a four-wheel-drive vehicle allows the Mowanjum community members to combine aspects of the traditional diet with the foods available in Derby, although at different times. It is also interesting to see that cattle formed the major component of their diet when they were living by hunting and gathering inland. The use of guns, and the fact that the cattle were theirs anyway, allowed them to substitute cattle for kangaroos and other smaller game. Under these circumstances there is no great need to use fire as a hunting tool — indeed it may well be counterproductive. However, the fact that they run a cattle station clearly demonstrates that they have chosen a very different lifestyle balance from the people living on the outstations in Arnhem Land.

The Mowanjum people also utilise the offshore islands, and to reach them they use dinghies and outboard motors, which have totally replaced the traditional watercraft of the region. Sue O'Connor suggests that 'today camping trips to the offshore islands are made for multifarious reasons and for varying durations. They may be as short as a single day trip or "picnic" or for prolonged periods of several weeks."[12]

The reasons for the trips may relate to renewing ties with traditional country, escaping the hustle of community living, hunting turtle and dugong, or obtaining trochus shell which is sold commercially. Woman and children will hunt fish in the tidal reef pools, collect fruit and dig yams. Men will use metal-tipped spears to catch turtle and large fish in deeper water from the bow of the dinghy. A great deal of time is spent sitting and chatting. Sometimes a cut-down 44-gallon drum will be left on a particular island for trochus food processing. In all cases, all of the activities are located close to the beach. O'Connor believes that the way the islands are used today is probably exactly the same way they were used before the advent of aluminium boats and outboard motors. However, there is a much greater ease of access with these resources, and the attraction of trochus shell which can be sold for cash provides an additional stimulus.[13]

A few hundred kilometres to the south of Derby, the Martujarra people of the Little Sandy Desert maintain a far greater use of traditional plant foods. Martujarra women dig tubers from the ground using both a traditional digging stick and a shovel, and *Cyperus* bulbs are similarly dug up and stored in plastic dishes. In these cases, European tools like shovels and plastic dishes are replacing their traditional wooden counterparts. Peter Veth and Fiona Walsh suggest that tubers of *Ipomoea* are a favourite bush tucker of people who live in Jigalong. *Acacia* seeds, particularly green ones, and grass seeds also still form part of the traditional diet.[14]

Twelve different fruits are eaten, and the *Santalum* and *Solanum* species are common in spinifex areas which have been burnt less than five years previously, so fire is still an important component of their socioeconomic system. The Martujarra retain the social context of gathering, and use a balance of bush foods and bought foods, both of which are available in the vicinity of their community.[15]

Richard Fullagar and Lesley Head worked in 1987 and 1988 with the Marralam community in the northwest of the Northern Territory, close to the Western Australian border. Two early dry seasons, a late dry season and a wet season were spent with the community. The land use by the community was of interest to them, so each trip which was undertaken from the base camp was detailed. Most of the trips were by four-wheel-drive vehicles, with the exception of a few trips in December 1987 which were by foot and can best be described as 'multipurpose' trips. At this time the roads were cut a few kilometres either side of Marralam, so vehicles could not be used.[16]

Most of the travelling was undertaken during the three dry-season periods, with travel being severely limited during the wet season. The dry-season trips included visits to rocky hills, alluvial flats, freshwater swamps and estuaries. Virtually all trips were based on roads or tracks, including several trips to Kununurra for shopping. A total of thirteen trips were undertaken in 64 days. Fires were lit adjacent to the main roads on several trips, primarily in the early dry season, for a range of reasons — easier access, better hunting, and to promote new growth.[17]

Most traditional food which was consumed was meat. Once again, plant food consumption was relatively minor. The solitary exception was on one occasion when bush mangoes were ripe, and they were enjoyed by everyone, but they were basically regarded as a snack rather than a staple. When bush meat could not be caught because of the weather conditions, tinned meat substituted.

Meat, birds and fish are highly prized, and access to bush meat is regarded as an important factor in the quality of life. In situations where the Marralam residents could not consume or store a particularly abundant catch (both bullocks and fish are mentioned), the surplus was taken to 'the poor starving people in town' (relatives in Kununurra). Kangaroos and turkeys which were shot on the way to town were generally given to the town dwellers. 'So as well as a regular transfer of store food from town to bush, there is a minor transfer in the opposite direction.'[18]

'Despite the apparent increase in sedentism provided by houses, community mobility is high, and resource use is spread across a number of different areas.'[19]

There is an increasing amount of time being spent on arts and craft for sale, and a number of trips were made specifically to collect wood for didgeridus, coolomons and clapsticks. Many people saw this as their 'work'. In 1990, when a vehicle payment was due, the whole community was involved in making arts and crafts for several days to make enough money.[20]

There is also a trend to visit favoured hunting places which had not be generally available because of the problem of transport. One spot was visited in 1990 for the first time in 30 years.[21]

Head and Fullagar summarise this way:

> In terms of potential impact on the environment, the evidence presented here is still preliminary. The impression at Marralam is that present predation levels are not detrimental, and that the restricted wet season access allows recovery, although it may also increase the pressure in the immediate vicinity of the camp, accessible on foot... At some point

people hunting from a sedentary base with guns will have a detrimental effect on replacement levels.[22]

The collection of specific kinds of wood for artefact manufacture is another possible impact, although the extent to which this may adversely effect the local environment is difficult to assess.

An interesting difference between the Marralam community and the Arnhem Land communities is that at Marralam there is no prohibition against women hunting with guns. When no men were available to hunt, women would do so. Only bullocks and flying foxes were hunted only by the men.[23]

One of the important things to come out of this discussion is the fact that Aboriginal people living in remote communities are heavily dependent on motor vehicles for access to a range of resources, both traditional and shop-bought. If communities or individuals are to own cars or trucks, then these have to be bought and maintained, and therefore there needs to be a source of cash income for the communities. Roads and tracks need to be maintained. Petrol costs are enormous for remote communities and it has been calculated that each person living in the Pitjantjatja Lands pays an average of $151 per year just in petrol tax.[24] Robert Lawrence reviewed the situation and suggests that 'Government policy towards transport will significantly determine the future of remote Aboriginal communities'.[25] He suggested that rationalisation of vehicle use was necessary. Conservationists have been telling white Australians the same thing for the last 30 years, without a great deal of success.

In summary then, different contemporary Aboriginal communities have chosen or been forced to adopt particular strategies for retaining aspects of traditional culture and at the same time utilising the advantages and benefits of a modern technology. In some instances, the balance may consist of living on an outstation, relying heavily on bush foods, but replacing the tedious job of digging and processing roots and tubers with earning cash to buy flour and sugar. In most communities, there is a strong recognition that hunting forms an important focus both economically and socially, and in some areas the role of women has shifted to include hunting activities. Firing the landscape remains an important traditional link with the past, and one which continues to have relevance.

The availability of boats and four-wheel-drive vehicles has meant that longer or more difficult trips can now be made more frequently and more easily, but the trade-off is that communities need to be able to acquire cash to buy and maintain vehicles and to pay for petrol. This may take the form of creating arts and crafts, collecting trochus shell, running cattle, or even receiving mining royalties. Where people would once walk to a favoured camping spot, in many cases they will now drive. Vehicle tracks cause much more localised damage than walking tracks. Trees are being cut down to make didgeridus and wooden artefacts for sale to tourists.

Many Aboriginal people are now having exactly the same kinds of impacts on the Australian environment as non-Aboriginal Australians.

CHAPTER 10

Conclusions

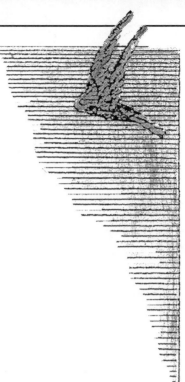

Land managers or exploiters?

The activities of Aboriginal people have caused some changes in the Australian environment. There have been vegetation changes through the use of fire, the selective dispersal of some plant species, hill-slope instability and in-filling of valleys, the digging of channels to join swamps, the creation of stone building and fish traps, the use of marginal areas through increased social networking, the adoption of specialised techniques for hunting certain types of animals and for catching fish, and the possible impact on populations of indigenous animals associated with the introduction of the dingo. Do these processes represent land management practices or do they in fact constitute exploitation of the landscape at the expense of the natural environment? This question has biological, social, economic and political implications.

There is a fine line which distinguished land management from land exploitation. Essentially, management involves the utilisation of the landscape without any long-term deterioration, whereas exploitation involves long-term degradation to the detriment of the environment. To use a simple but appropriate analogy, contemporary European Australians clearly are exploiters, not managers. However, a mosaic of 'exploitation' exists. The modern population centres are clear examples of a disastrous impact; because the land is denuded of trees and a great deal of infrastructure is built up. In rural areas; trees are cleared, pastures improved or altered, and as a consequence the land is frequently degraded. The problems of overstocking, soil erosion, excessive use of pesticides and herbicides, open-cut mining, reduction in suitable habitat for animal species, eutrophication of the waterways, and air pollution, are all aspects of the contemporary industrialised Australian society which are clearly objectionable from an environmental perspective. This is exploitation of the landscape, because it results in long-term degradation. However, Australia does have wild areas, National Parks, uninhabited deserts and untouched stretches of coastline, so what we observe is a mosaic of European environmental impact.

Having accepted that the present population of Australian exploit the landscape, but not necessarily all of it, and that they do so to a different extent in different places, are we really saying that it is not just the nature of land use which is the problem, but the intensity of land use, which is related to the human population density, and which in turn determines the extent of contemporary human impact on the Australian environment? Clearly population density is an important component of any discussion on human environmental impacts. The same argument could be used for Aboriginal impact on Australia — the impact is small if the population is small, but the impact increases as the population increases.

It could be argued that any human occupation will result in exploitation and therefore degradation of the landscape. If one accepts that humans are part of the living world, and have a role to play within that world, then surely the interaction between humans and their environment is a 'natural' phenomenon. The issue is that virtually all modern human societies, because of their high population density and social and economic infrastructure, will use up resources at an ever increasing rate, and therefore cause land degradation simply because there are more people to support.

I would argue then that there are two main interrelated factors which determine whether land-use practices can be defined as management or exploitation. The first is the nature of the land-use strategy and the second is the human population density. Both of these factors may seem intuitively obvious, but they need to be justified because of the implications for our understanding of traditional and contemporary Aboriginal societies and the nature of their impact on the environment.

Once the process of agriculture and herding began, perhaps 10,000 years ago, there was no turning back because, in order to support the greater density of population, a system of land management was needed which ensured the regular availability of large quantities of food to feed the growing localised population in the settlements.

This step is crucial, because it meant that populations which adopted agriculture as their economic base no longer had the option of returning to a hunting and gathering lifestyle, which by definition has a lesser impact on the environment.

Human population has expanded enormously over the last 8,000 years, but the rate of growth has not been constant. As agriculture increased, so did the population density, and with the exception of the period when bubonic plague ravaged the world, human populations have continued to increase ever since. However, with the technological advances of the industrial revolution, the rate of growth of the world's population has increased enormously.

In tracing the history of Aboriginal people in Australia, we have seen that the Aboriginal population density also appeared to increase dramatically, particularly during the last 5000 years. We saw that mechanisms were developed to increase the productivity of the landscape, albeit within the context of a hunter-gatherer economy. Eel traps, replanting yams and regular burning all increased the availability of resources, which was necessary in order to feed a growing Aboriginal population. There is no need to enter into the circular argument of which came first, the increasing population or the more productive land management practices. There is ample evidence that these two processes both occurred within Aboriginal Australia over the last 5000 years, so the factors which resulted in farmers and herders beginning to 'exploit' the landscape rather than 'manage' it were present in Australia before European settlement.

Once land management practices were adopted by Aboriginal people to increase the productivity of the landscape, then there were pressures on their communities to maintain the environments they had created in order to feed the growing population. If you like, once the carrying capacity of the land had been increased, then there were no opportunities to revert to an 'unimproved' environment. The people needed to be fed. If this is the case, then we must accept that the environment which confronted Europeans in 1788 was one which was managed, and which was certainly different from what Australia would have been like without Aboriginal land-management practices. That is not to say that there would have been any major obvious physical differences. The biogeographical history of Australia determined the range of plant and animal species which would occur within the region, but the balance and distribution of species had been altered by Aboriginal involvement, most obviously by the use of fire.

If this hypothesis is correct, then the next question we must ask ourselves is: why didn't Aboriginal people adopt the kinds of management processes which were adopted by farmers and herders in other parts of the world? Why was there no agriculture, herding, permanent villages or the use of metals? At least some of the answers are fairly obvious. The semi-arid grasslands of Australia had irregular rainfall, long periods of drought and occasional flooding. The flat, dry, arid landscape simply was not suitable for farming suitable grasses, and the method of exploiting them was therefore largely opportunistic. In terms of herding, there are no animals indigenous to Australia which could have been domesticated. Wallabies and kangaroos are difficult if not impossible to control, require a range of microhabitats, and need large territories to exploit. Herding was simply not an option with the range of animal resources available. However, there are examples of settlements which appear to have been, if not permanent, then at least of a long duration of occupation.

Essentially, over much of Australia the environment simply did not allow the development of the kinds of farming and herding practices which had developed in other parts of the world. This is apparent when you see how many modern Australian farmers are finding that they cannot be economically viable, even though they have all the modern technological aids available to them.

Based on the nature of traditional Aboriginal society, the land-management practices did not have any particularly serious long-term adverse effects, although it is worth remembering that in some sensitive areas like the Hawkesbury sandstone country around Sydney, regular burning did result in destabilisation of the hill slopes and changing impacts in the valley floors and perhaps lower down the rivers and creeks. In general, Aboriginal people were land managers, not land exploiters.

When we talk about conservation of the Australian environment, what are we really talking about? Do we mean conserving the environment as it was in 1788 — an environment which was created as a result of the interaction with Aboriginal people — or do we mean conserving the environment as it develops in the absence of regular, routine, low-intensity burning; or do we mean conserving it in the absence of the dingo; or in the absence of foxes and feral cats; or in the absence of the rabbit, the goat, the pig, the camel and the donkey; or do we mean conserving it without any human impact whatsoever — by excluding people altogether from National Parks?

One important development to come out of these questions is the growing involvement of Aboriginal people in the management of National Parks. In both Kakudu and Uluru, the traditional Aboriginal owners now have an opportunity to assist in the decision making about things like the frequency and location of burning, and the visitation levels.

While this is an important step forward, it is also important to remember that there have been changes in the environment which are irreversible. Once an animal is extinct, it is gone for ever, and no amount of land-management practice adopted in retrospect will change that. Most feral animals have already made a dramatic impact, and short of some amazing biological control mechanism, that impact will remain. Indeed, even Aboriginal people now have quite different impacts on the environment, even when they are still living in traditional communities. Boats, cars, trucks and guns have all changed Aboriginal land-use practices, although there are some locations, such as outstations, where these changes may be minimal. Burning regimes are not the same as they were 200 years ago; rifles are used to hunt, not spears; boats and nets are used to catch fish, not canoes and lines; outboard motors erode creek banks, where bark canoes do not.

Aboriginal culture has changed as a result of contact with European society, and one hopes inappropriate European land-management practices can be influenced by traditional Aboriginal culture. One of the most contentious issues is whether or not Aboriginal burning patterns should be used as a modern tool for land management.

To burn or not to burn?

It is clear that fire is an important component of the Australian environment. There are many changes which can result from an area burning, and mosaics of vegetation can develop when burning is undertaken in different times. Another aspect of the impact of burning is the frequency with which it takes place. The rate of burning will determine the characteristics and species composition of a particular piece of landscape.

Before considering the contribution of Aboriginal burning to the Australian environment, we must first look at the natural frequency of fires in different vegetation associations. Walker has published a map showing expected fire frequencies in different fire season regions, with the frequency expressed as a range of years.[1] In Northern Australia, natural fires are to be expected every one to two years, whereas in the Sydney area, fires are expected every five to twelve years. There are factors which influence these ranges, such as the amount of clearing, development, and population density. Sydney, Melbourne and Alice Springs all have higher than expected fire frequencies compared with other areas of the same climate and vegetation types because of their high population density.

Fire is common in grassy communities, but rare in brigalow and rainforests. On the mainland, most areas will burn at least once every

50 years and in Tasmania, because of the greater rainfall and cooler conditions, the frequency is even less. Tasmanian sclerophyll forests will burn around once every 100 years, and rainforests might be expected to burn on average around once every 300 years.[2]

That some animals are adapted to frequent fires has been clearly demonstrated. The native mouse, *Pseudomys novaehollandiae*, was believed extinct, but was rediscovered in heath regenerating after fire.[3] One *Pseodomys* species was found to be dependent on heaths with the maximum diversity of woody plants, which was reached eight to ten years after a fire, and both the plant diversity and the mouse population declined thereafter.[4] Evidence exists from sub-fossil deposits that the group were widespread and common until recent times. Cockburn suggested that the presumed reduction in fire frequency since European settlement may have led to the decline of species diversity of the pseudomyine rodents as a whole.[5]

The rat kangaroo, *Bettongia penicillata*, is almost certainly a fire specialist. This species prefers thickets of *Casuarina* for shelter, and that habitat requires fires every seven years or so to be maintained. However, short-term population reductions have been observed immediately after fire due to predation by foxes and native cats, almost certainly because of increased exposure and reduced shelter.

Some birds, including the lyrebird, favour areas that have been burnt, and at least one species of ground parrot has recently become rare almost certainly because of a reduction in the frequency of fire.[7]

The pattern of biomass change following fire has been observed for a range of small mammals at Nadgee in southern New South Wales following the 1972 fire. Different species responded at different rates in different environments, but the overall pattern was similar.[8] Work conducted by Fox in the Myall Lake area demonstrates a remarkably similar pattern to that observed in Nadgee. The mice tend to peak around two years after a fire, while the rats and small carnivorous marsupials take longer.[9]

If we look at the biology of the possums, we find that there seems to be a correlation between the frequency of fire in the environments they occupy and their breeding potential. Greater gliders live in the upper canopy of wet sclerophyll forests, which burn infrequently. They have a low reproductive potential (0.6 young per year) and have the best defined and shortest breeding season of the possums. Ringtail and brush-tail possums, which live in the lower levels of dry sclerophyll forests, an environment much more likely to burn, have longer and less well defined breeding seasons and a fecundity that is two to three times that of the glider. In the brush-tail, the breeding season also seems to be influenced by the fire-proneness of the habitat. In the wetter habitats of Tasmania, most births occur in the autumn, but in the drier areas like Sydney and Canberra, breeding occurs in both seasons.[10]

The honey possum, which lives in extremely fire-prone *Banksia* heaths in southwestern Western Australia, has no defined breeding season, and reproduction is opportunistic, almost certainly as a consequence of the frequent fires which occur.

Amongst the macropods, breeding also seems to be related to the likelihood of fire. In Tasmania, red-necked wallabies breed seasonally, but in the more flammable mainland forests they breed all year round.[12]

It has been suggested that those animals best suited to a fire-prone environment would be generalists, with a broad diet and the flexibility to adjust according to the availability of various food items. Interestingly, from the work at Nadgee, the dingo appears to be the best suited carnivorous animal for coping with a fire-prone environment. The small mammals were rare in the first year after fire, so the dingoes switched to large game. In periods when few prey species were available in 1974 after the fire, *Solanum* fruits were eaten, but not in 1971, 1972, 1973, 1975 or 1976. When the waterbirds came into the lake the dingoes ate them.[13] It is interesting to speculate if the Thylacine and *Sarcophilus*, the devil, were adapted to fire-prone regimes. If not, this could be another reason why the dingo succeeded in an environment where Aborigines were burning regularly.

Of the tree-dwelling, animals, the ringtail possum, which is much broader in its herbiverous diet than the greater glider, can be considered a successful generalist. In fact, most of the animals which live in the woodlands and sclerophyll forest have broader diets than those specialists which live in rainforests and wet sclerophyll forests which burn rarely. It seems that certain characteristics of diet, reproductive strategy and habitat selection are strongly influenced by fire frequency, and those animals which succeed in the scerophyll forests are those which have evolved along with regular fires.[14]

What is the implication for the forest mammals if Aborigines dramatically increase the frequency of fires? Clearly, different animals will be impacted in different ways. Let us take a hypothetical area of scerophyll vegetation. If Aborigines burn the area, one year later the kangaroos and wallabies will be present in large numbers, because they reach their peak within a year and decline thereafter. (However, after an extreme and widespread crown fire, the macropod population could take several years to recover.) The population of rats and mice will be low; the population of possums would not be significantly affected; nor would the population of wombats or of dingoes.

By two years after the fire, macropod populations would be declining but rats and mice would be increasing, with the mice peaking at about two years. The longer the area goes unburnt, the greater the decline in macropods, the greater the decline in mice, and the greater the increase in rats.

The trend is apparent and consistent — with some animals declining, some increasing, and some like the possums and wombats remaining fairly constant.

So if Aborigines wanted to maximise the productivity of the landscape, what strategy should they adopt? The animals in the sclerophyll forests are adapted to fires and will survive them. Woodlands and forests can be burnt regularly without any long-term decline in the fauna, and if it is burnt every one to three years the macropod population will be kept near the sustainable maximum level. On the other hand, it would be unwise to burn wet sclerophyll and rainforests because the animals in those vegetation association tend to be specialists, not well-adapted to fire. If you want to protect those animals, you don't burn the rainforests.

If you want to maximise the biomass and retain the diversity of the animals and indeed birds in an area, a mosaic pattern of burning, with most woodland areas burnt every one to three years, but with the wet sclerophyll and rainforests burnt less frequently, if at all, would seem to be the most successful strategy.

What would the impact of this fire regime be on the flora? It would be essentially the same. The vegetation would be in a state of flux, but there would be a high diversity, and certain species would be favoured in the recently burnet areas — lilies and orchids for tubers, burrawang for seeds, *Banksia* and *Grevillea* for nectar, etc. In those wetter areas which do not burn, fruits which grow on established trees will be favoured.

It is important to consider the impact of regular burning on wet sclerophyll forests and rainforest margins. These areas are characterised by regular and high rainfall and they are often sheltered from the worst dessication of fire-promoting winds. When a wet sclerophyll forest does burn, it is characterised by rapid regeneration soon after the fire. In *Eucalyptus regnans* forests, half of the final height can be achieved in 25 years.[15] There is an interesting relationship between rainfall and fire. The greater the rainfall the greater the amount of fuel to burn, and therefore the more intense the fires, but the less frequently fires are likely to occur.

In the years immediately following a fire it is not uncommon to find that there is a luxurient growth of herbs, in much the same way as in the dry sclerophyll forests, but in the wet sclerophyll these are rapidly overtaken by the regeneration of trees and shrubs. The species diversity is greater a year or two after fire, and can actually double in *Eucalyptus diversicolor* forests. Yet many of the species are fire-sensitive, but they still require occasional fire to reproduce.[16] Wet sclerophyll should therefore burn occasionally but not too often. Put more correctly, wet sclerophyll will burn occasionally regardless of whether Aborigines or natural sources of ignition start the fire.

If wet sclerophyll forest burns frequently, there will be a change in the species composition. Fire-adapted dry sclerophyll will increase, the nutrient levels of the soil will decrease, and these factors will contribute to an increase in fire frequency. This in turn promotes fire-adapted species.

In heathlands, the plant species diversity decreases rapidly since the last fire. A long-term study carried out on Park Island, in South Australia, showed that diversity declined from 39 species immediately after fire to 11 species in areas that had not burnt for 50 years. Most seedlings emerge within a year following fire, but no new seedlings are found between five and fifteen years after fire. Heath is clearly a dynamic ecosystem, which burns regularly, and which is not adversely impacted by frequent burning.[17]

One of the most sensitive vegetation associations is the spinifex country of the arid zone, mostly dominated by *Triodia*. The natural fire regime consists of summer burns every one to five years, but the frequency was probably increased slightly by the Aborigines. European land-use patterns in this country involved winter burns, which promoted the *Triodia* at the expense of more nutritious grasses. Euros could thrive on this diet but sheep couldn't. Euro numbers increased and reinforced the change to poorer quality vegetation. In one study undertaken during the 1950s, the population of euros averaged 40 per square km. It was not until the euro numbers were reduced, and summer burns reinstigated, that the grass returned and the land once again became suitable for sheep.[18]

Hazard-reduction burning

We seem to have answered a number of questions about the relationship between Aborigines and fire. Aborigines used fire, particularly in those environments which were adapted to fire. The frequency of burning may have increased, and mosaic patterns of vegetation resulted from the way Aborigines burned, but essentially the areas which were not fire-adapted burnt infrequently and the fire-adapted areas burned more frequently. The impact on the vegetation was probably to maximise the plant diversity and maintain non-climax communities in many areas like the spinifex country, heath, woodland and dry sclerophyll forests. The consequence was that large animals like kangaroos and wallabies were favoured, and possums and wombats were little affected. The frequency and seasonality of Aboriginal burning ensured that the vegetation associations generated by Aboriginal burning, at least over the last few thousand years, were maintained.

Then along came Europeans. Aboriginal burning regimes changed. Fires were no longer routine. Some burning took place in the wrong season. Some areas were left unburnt, allowing an accumulation of fuel, and when a fire did occur it was a crown fire, destroying the forests. European land-management practices could not tolerate the possibility that crown fires might develop and destroy the infrastructure which was necessary to run a property. A new tool was introduced — hazard-reduction burning. Areas of land were intentionally burnt to reduce the accumulation of fuel and to ensure that a crown fire did not develop.

What are the consequences of this new fire regime? It depends on the vegetation association. Grasslands, woodlands and sclerophyll forests are used to fires, and it doesn't really matter if the fire occurs every three or four years or every ten years. Indeed, some forests in Tasmania have probably not burnt for several hundred years. The critical thing is maintaining the diversity, including the old-growth forests. If these mature forests are burnt more frequently than they were under an Aboriginal fire regime, it seems likely that dry sclerophyll vegetation will be favoured. The answer seems to be — don't burn the tall forest and rainforest margins too often, the critical problem being the definition of 'too often'.

The consequences for the fauna of changing fire regimes is also apparent. The shift from summer fires to winter fires in the spinifex country changed the nature of the vegetation and consequently the fauna. Small mammals seem to have been impacted most severely. As long as the fires are not too frequent in the woodlands and dry sclerophyll forests, and provided there is a mosaic of vegetation maintained by varying the frequency of fires in different areas, the burning pattern in these areas would not seem to be critical. However, the fire-sensitive animals are those which occur in the tall forest, wet sclerophyll forests and rainforests, and an increase in the fire frequency in these areas is likely to have an impact on the specialised animals which occupy those specialised niches.

Perhaps decisions about hazard-reduction burning needs to take into account the reasons for burning. The reasons Aboriginal people used fire related to increasing the productivity of the landscape to support their relatively high population density. Fire would not be routinely and regularly used unless there was a particular need for it. The Gunei in Arnhem Land do not burn for nine or ten months of the year because they are pyromaniacs, they burn to increase the productivity of the landscape.[19] Fire is used for immediate hunting, to promote food plants and animals in the future, and to make travel easier. These things are only necessary if food is scarce, or might be scarce, or people need to travel over distances. The intensive use of fire, so ubiquitous in Aboriginal culture, tells us that Aboriginal populations were exploiting the landscape to the best of their ability, supporting the greatest human population density, ensuring a constant supply of food both in the present and in the future, and facilitating movement across the landscape to allow these other things to happen.

Coupled with the archaelogical data which confirm that Aboriginal populations had increased dramatically over the last 5000 years, and which demonstrate that important technological changes had occurred, it is apparent that a diverse range of resources was being exploited, and a component of this process was the 'artificial' increase in some animals at the expense of others by habitat modification. Aboriginal use of fire changed the balance, but not the essential character, of Australia's flora and fauna.

When modern hazard-reduction burning is undertaken, the function of the burn is to reduce the amount of litter and understorey vegetation in order to reduce the likelihood of wildfires developing. The reason this is done usually has nothing to do with the impact of the fire on the vegetation. Rather, it is to protect homes and other infrastructure from the threat of destruction. Hazard-reduction burns have a different function from Aboriginal burning, and any argument that suggests that Aboriginal fire regimes should be reintroduced totally ignores this fact.[20]

Before European settlement, the Aboriginal population of Australia was not evenly dispersed. Probably the greatest population density was along the southeast coast and along the Murray–Darling River system. We might therefore expect that these would be the areas which would be most affected by Aboriginal activities. However, they are probably not the most environmentally sensitive areas. In the southeast, the sclerophyll vegetation was pre-adapted to fire, which was relatively common. In parts of central Australia, the communities might burn once every 50 years, due to natural sources of ignition, but perhaps every one to two years due to Aboriginal burning. Such a dramatic increase in fire frequency could also have a dramatic impact on both animal communities and vegetation associations.

In the semi-arid zone, once Aboriginal burning stopped there was a dramatic increase in 'woody weeds' — shrubs which replaced the

grassland communities. It is fair to say that, without Aboriginal burning, the area would have been dominated by a very different range of
plant species. Indeed, it has been suggested that the grassland and
woodland communities generated and sustained by Aboriginal burning were an artefact of human activities, and therefore Aboriginal
people should be viewed as an important and integral component to
the Australian ecosystem as it existed in 1788.

There is little point in speculating what the ecosystem would
have been like without the Aboriginal people, even though palaeontologists like David Horton argue that it would have been little different.[21] I do not agree with this point of view. I think the evidence
weighs heavily towards the view that, at the time of European occupation, Aboriginal people possessed a diverse range of technological
adaptions which maximised the productivity of the landscape in order
to support a high population density. I also believe that additional
technological changes would not only have been likely to occur, but
necessary. Put in simple terms, Aboriginal society was in a state of
growth and development it was not capable of sustaining by using the
range of social and technological tools available to it.

This is not a value judgment. I do not suggest that this is a good or
bad thing. Indeed, how do we decide if it is better to have a lot of kangaroos or a lot of possums or wet sclerophyll forest or open woodlands?
The European view of the world, from the point of view of the conservationists at least, would probably argue that we should maintain biodiversity. It is likely that traditional Aboriginal land-management
practices did contribute to maintaining species diversity. But we must
recognise that Aboriginal people in 1788 were not viewing Australia
from the perception of middle-class, suburban, white Australians in
the 1990s. They were surviving, successfully, and doing so by manipu-
lating the environment, just as twentieth century non-Aboriginal
Australians manipulate the environment to support their biological
needs and their cultural wants and desires.

Contemporary communities

Where does this leave contemporary Aboriginal communities which
continue to maintain socioeconomic links with their land. Clearly
they have a different range of biological and cultural needs and
desires from their ancestors in 1788. They have the right to have
access to any technolgical advancement which modern European
society can offer them — medicines, education, transportation systems, even television if they want it. There will be changes in
Aboriginal land tenure, particularly in the light of the Mabo decision

and Native Title legislation.[22] It is important to recognise that Aboriginal communities should have the right to practise their religious and cultural beliefs, provided they do not threaten the biological diversity we have retained. It seems incongruous that while kangaroo-shooters were shooting more than a million kangaroos a year in Queensland in the 1960s and 1970s for dog food, an Aboriginal man could be prosecuted and jailed for hunting a kangaroo. However, conservationists might take a different attitude if an Aboriginal man wanted to hunt and kill one of the last banded hare wallabies in existence. There is clearly room for compromise and, indeed, Aboriginal conservation mechanisms like totemism and food prohibitions are designed for exactly the same conservation purposes as some of the non-Aboriginal legislation.

Aboriginal people want to sustain their cultural and social beliefs. This means conservation of the plants and animals which make up that belief system, and to suggest that Aborigines had no impact on their environment is to deny their place in Australia's ecological history.

Put simply, there are many differences between Aboriginal and European land-use practices. They achieve different ends. They use different methodologies. Both can cause large-scale and long-term modification to the environment. Both can cause animal and plant extinctions, but these are far more likely under European land-management practices. Some European practices like open-cut mining and forestry are destructive, and it might take many generations for the land to recover. Aboriginal land management practices might cause disturbance, but recovery is likely to be within a single generation or at most a few generations (extinctions aside, of course).

Finally, the Australia that we are all living in is a product of 50,000 of Aboriginal land use and 205 years of European land use. I will let you judge which culture has had the greater impact.

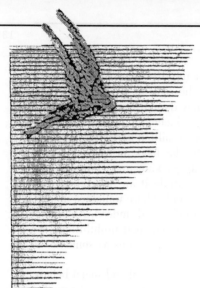

Endnotes

Introduction

1 White and O'Connell (1982) pp 63–4
2 Horton (1980)
3 Jones (1969)
4 Mitchell (1848) p 412
5 Flannery (1990)

Chapter 1

1 Pyne (1991) p 2
2 ibid p 4
3 Kershaw (1986)
4 Pyne (1991)
5 Archer et al (1991)
6 Gollan (1984)
7 Archer and Clayton (1984)
8 ibid
9 White and O'Connell (1982)

Chapter 2

1 Lewin (1991)
2 Thorne and Raymond (1989) p 18
3 ibid p 35–6
4 Stringer (1990); Wilson and Cann (1992)
5 Bar-Yosef and Vandermeersch (1993)

6 Thorn and Raymond (1989); Thorne and Wolpoff (1992)
7 ibid
8 ibid
9 Allen et al (1977)
10 Roberts et al (1990)
11 Pearce and Barbetti (1981)
12 Coutts (1978)
13 Claims for early sites in Victoria have not been substantiated.
14 Thorne and Macumber (1972)
15 Freedman and Lofgren (1979)
16 Brown (1989); Dayton (1994)
17 Brown (1981)
18 Thorne and Raymond (1989)
19 Cosgrove (1989)
20 Schrire (1982)
21 Bowdler (1977)
22 Martin and Klein (1984)
23 Birdsell (1977)
24 Bowdler (1984)
25 Smith (1989)
26 White and O'Connell (1982)
27 ibid
28 Macknight (1976)

Chapter 3

1 Veth (1989)
2 Cosgrove (1989)
3 ibid
4 Kiernan et al (1983)
5 Allen (1989)
6 Jones (1971)
7 ibid
8 White and O'Connell (1982)
9 Bowdler (1984)
10 Vanderwal (1978)
11 Thomas (1993)
12 Stockton (1970); Stockton and Holland (1974)
13 Kohen et al (1984)
14 Stockton and Holland (1974)
15 Nanson et al (1987); Kohen (in prep)
16 McCarthy (1964)
17 Flood (1980)
18 Flood et al (1987)
19 Bowdler (1976); Lampert (1971a)
20 Chappell and Grinrod (1981)
21 Kefous (1977)
22 Smith (1986)
23 Smith (1986); Veth (1989)
24 Smith et al (1993)
25 Pocock (1988)
26 Veth (1989)
27 ibid

Chapter 4

1 Horton (1982) p 237
2 Singh et al (1981)
3 Kershaw (1993)
4 Clark (1983) p 35
5 Beaton (1982)
6 Singh et al (1981) p 33
7 Singh and Geissler (1985)
8 Singh et al (1981) p 44
9 Kershaw (1993)
10 Clark (1983)
11 Head (1989)
12 Wright (1986b)
13 Horton (1982)

14 Pyne (1991)
15 Hughes and Sullivan (1981)
16 Hickin and Page (1971)
17 Clark and McLoughlin (1986)
18 Kodela and Dodson (1988)
19 Jones (1969)
20 Cunningham (1827)
21 Phillip (1789)
22 Benson and Howell (1990)
23 Pyne (1991)

Chapter 5

1 Flannery (1990)
2 Lampert (1981, 1983a); Wright (1986a)
3 Draper (1987)
4 Wright (1986a)
5 White and O'Connell (1982)
6 Archer (1984)
7 Vartanyan et al (1993); Lister (1989)
8 Martin and Klein (1984)
9 ibid
10 Gollan (1984)
11 Wright (1986a)
12 ibid
13 Vickers-Rich et al (1991); Wright (1986a)
14 Tindale-Biscoe (1975)
15 Gorecki et al (1984)
16 Palmer (1993); Dodson et al (1993)
17 Horton (1980)
18 Horton (1981)
19 Veth (1989)
20 ibid
21 Wright (1986a); Dodson et al (1993)
22 Horton (1981)
23 Caughley et al (1980)
24 Vickers-Rich et al (1991)
25 Flannery and Gott (1983)
26 Lampert (1981)
27 ibid
28 Dodson et al (1993)
29 Kershaw (1986)
30 Clark (1983)

31 Jones (1969)
32 Clark (1983)
33 Flannery (1990)
34 White and O'Connell (1982) p 94
35 Archer et al (1980)
36 Saul (1992), p 14
37 Winter (1970)
38 Bowman (1991)
39 Flannery (1990); Martin and Klein (1984)
40 Flannery (1990); Horton (1980)
41 Flannery and Gott (1983)
42   J. Peter White, pers. comm.

Chapter 6

1   Clark (1978)
2   Campbell (1993)
3   Martin and Klein (1984)
4   Richard Venables, pers. comm.
5   Winter (1970)
6   Darwin (1845) p 202
7   Meehan (1982)
8   ibid
9   ibid
10 Meggitt (1962)
11 Meehan (1982)
12 ibid pp 159–60
13 ibid
14 Isaacs (1987) p 93
15 Schrire (1982)
16 Mulvaney (1975)
17 White and O'Connell (1982)
18 ibid
19 Hughes and Lampert (1982)
20 White and O'Connell (1982)
21 ibid
22 Wright (1986a)
23 Tindale (1937)
24 Lampert (1981)
25 ibid
26 ibid
27 Wright (1986a)
28 Flood (1983)
29 Schrire (1982)
30 Lampert (1983a)
31 Kamminga (1978)
32 Flood (1983)

33 ibid p 50
34 ibid
35 ibid
36 ibid p 49
37 ibid
38 Leubbers (1975)
39 Mulvaney (1975)
40 Dickson (1981)
41 Lampert (1971b)
42 Clarke (1994)
43 White and O'Connell (1982)
44 Lourandos (1983)
45 ibid
46 Lampert and Hughes (1980)
47 Ross (1981)
48 Hughes and Lampert (1982)
49 Clark (1978)
50 Cohen (1977) pp 78–83
51 Kohen and Lampert (1987)
52 Kohen (1986)
53 Beaton (1982)
54 Hughes and Sullivan (1981)
55 Brown (1989)
56 Sullivan (1976); Bowdler (1976)
57 Kohen (1986)
58 Banks (1770)

Chapter 7

1   Radcliffe-Brown (1930)
2   Butlin (1983)
3   Kohen (1988)
4   Lourandos (1977)
5   Lourandos (1983)
6   Lampert (1971b)
7   Meehan (1982)
8   White and O'Connell (1982)
9   Jones (1974)
10 Jones (1971)
11 Dodson (ed.) (1992)
12 Gollan (1984)
13 White and O'Connell (1982)
14 Guiler (1985)
15 Newsome and Catling (1983)
16 ibid
17 ibid
18 ibid

19 Caughley et al (1980)
20 Newsome et al (1983)
21 Martin (1994)
22 Guiler (1985)
23 Gollan (1984)
24 Macintosh (1971)
25 Archer et al (1991)
26 Winter (1970)
27 ibid
28 Frith and Calaby (1969)
29 Butlin (1983)
30 Kohen (1986, 1988)
31 Etheridge et al (1896)
32 Jones (1969)
33 Horton (1982); Wright (1986a)
34 Catling and Newsome (1981)
35 Pyne (1991)
36 Kohen (1985)
37 Flood (1983)
38 ibid p 208
39 ibid p 205
40 ibid p 208
41 ibid pp 205–6
42 Clarke (1994)
43 White and O'Connell (1982) p 155
44 Peterson (1986)
45 Flood (1983)
46 ibid
47 Goede and Murray (1977)
48 Hughes and Sullivan (1981)
49 Hughes (1980)
50 Hughes and Sullivan (1981) p 277
51 Hickin and Page (1971)
52 Blong and Gillespie (1978)
53 Singh et al (1981)
54 ibid
55 Lampert and Sanders (1973)
56 Kohen and Lampert (1987)
57 Flood (1980)
58 ibid
59 ibid
60 Brook and Kohen (1991)
61 Cohen (1977)
62 Lourandos (1983)
63 Veth (1989)
64 Marun (1972)
65 Lampert and Hughes (1980)
66 Smith (1989)
67 ibid
68 ibid
69 Veth (1989)
70 ibid

Chapter 8

1 Hallam (1975) p 12
2 Kohen (1988)
3 Kohen (1993)
4 Kohen (1985)
5 Pyne (1991) p 87
6 Hallam (1975)
7 Pyne (1991)
8 ibid
9 ibid p 123
10 ibid
11 ibid
12 Creagh (1992)
13 Pyne (1991)
14 Birckhead et al (1993)
15 Pyne (1991)
16 Clark (1983)
17 Specht (1981)
18 Noble and Slatyer (1981)
19 ibid p 314
20 ibid p 315
21 ibid
22 Catling and Newsome (1981)
23 ibid
24 ibid
25 Christensen and Kimber (1975)
26 Catling and Newsome (1981)
27 Christensen and Kimber (1975)
28 Guiler (1985)
29 ibid p 14
30 ibid p 11
31 ibid p 13
32 ibid p 28
33 Kohen (1986)

Chapter 9

1 *Native Title Act 1993* (Commonwealth)
2 Altman (1984)

3   Meehan (1982)
4   Altman (1984) p 37
5   ibid
6   ibid
7   ibid
8   ibid
9   ibid
10   O'Dea et al (1987)
11   ibid
12   O'Connor (1989)
13   ibid
14   Veth and Walsh (1988)
15   ibid
16   Head and Fullagar (1991)
17   ibid
18   ibid
19   ibid
20   ibid
21   ibid
22   ibid
23   Altman (1984)
24   Lawrence (1991)
25   ibid

Chapter 10
1   Walker (1981)
2   ibid
3   Catling and Newsome (1981)
4   ibid
5   ibid
6   ibid
7   ibid
8   ibid
9   Fox (1978)
10   Catling and Newsome (1981)
11   ibid
12   ibid
13   ibid
14   ibid
15   Ashton (1981)
16   ibid
17   Specht (1981)
18   Pyne (1991) pp 220–1
19   ibid
20   Birckhead et al (1993)
21   Horton (1982)
22   *Native Title Act 1993*
     (Commonwealth)

Bibliography

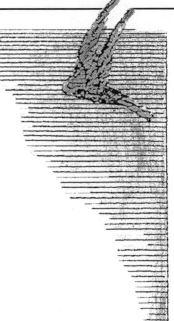

Allen, J. 1989. Excavations at Bone Cave, South Central Tasmania, January–February 1989. *Australian Archaeology* 28: 105–6.

Allen, J., J. Golson and R. Jones. 1977. *Sunda and Sahul. Prehistoric studies in Southeast Asia, Melanesia and Australia.* Academic Press, Sydney.

Altman, J.C. 1984. The dietary utilisation of flora and fauna by contemporary hunter-gatherers at Momega outstation, north-central Arnhem Land. *Australian Aboriginal Studies* 1984 No 1, pp 35–46.

Archer, M. 1984. Effects of humans on the Australian vertebrate fauna. In M. Archer and G. Clayton (eds.) *Vertebrate zoogeography — evolution in Australasia.* Hesperian Press, Carlisle, W.A.

Archer, M. and G. Clayton (eds.) 1984. *Vertebrate zoogeography — evolution in Australasia.* Hesperian Press, Carlisle, W.A.

Archer, M., I.M. Crawford and D. Merrilees. 1980. Incisions, breakages and charring, some probably man-made, in fossil bones from Mammoth Cave, Western Australia. *Alcheringa* 4: 115–131.

Archer, M., S.J. Hand and H. Godthelp. 1991. Riversleigh. *The story of animals in ancient rainforests of inland Australia.* Reed Books, Balgowlah.

Ashton, D.H. 1981. Fire in tall open forests (Wet sclerophyll forests). In A.M. Gill, R.H. Groves and I.R. Noble (eds). *Fire and the Australian biota.* Australian Academy of Science, Canberra.

Bailey, G.N. 1975. The role of molluscs in coastal economies: the results of midden analysis in Australia. *Journal of Archaeological Science* 2: 45–62.

Banks, J. 1770 (1962). In Beaglehole, J.C. (ed.) *The Endeavour journal of Joseph Banks 1768–1771.* Angus and Robertson, Sydney.

Bar-Yosef, O. and B. Vandermeersch. 1993. Modern humans in the Levant.

Scientific American April 1993, pp 64–70.

Barker, B.C. and A. Macintosh. 1979. The Dingo: a review. *Archaeology and Physical Anthropology in Oceania* 14: 27–53.

Beaton, J.M. 1982. Fire and water: aspects of Australian Aboriginal management of cycads. *Archaeology in Oceania* 17(1): 51–8.

Benson, D. and J. Howell. 1990. *Taken for granted. The bushland of Sydney and its suburbs.* Kangaroo Press in association with the Royal Botanic Gardens, Sydney.

Birckhead, J., T. De Lacy and L. Smith (eds) 1993. *Aboriginal involvement in parks and protected areas.* Australian Institute of Aboriginal and Torres Strait Islander Studies Report Series, Aboriginal Studies Press, Canberra.

Birdsell, J.B. 1977. The recalibration of a paradigm for the first peopling of greater Australia. In J. Allen, J. Golson and R. Jones (eds) *Sunda and Sahul. Prehistoric studies from Southeast Asia, Melanesia and Australia.* Academic Press, London.

Blong, R.J. and R. Gillespie. 1978. Fluvially transported charcoal gives erroneous ages for recent deposits. *Nature* 271: 739–41.

Bowdler, S. 1976. Hook, line and dilly bag: an interpretation of an Aboriginal coastal shell midden. *Mankind* 10: 248–58.

Bowdler, S. 1977. The coastal colonisation of Australia. In J. Allen, J. Golson and R. Jones (eds) *Sunda and Sahul. Prehistoric studies from Southeast Asia, Melanesia and Australia.* Academic Press, London.

Bowdler, S. 1981. Hunters in the highlands: Aboriginal adaptations in the eastern Australian uplands. *Archaeology in Oceania* 16: 99–111.

Bowdler, S. 1984. Hunter Hill, Hunter Island. *Terra Australis* 8, Department of Prehistory, Research School of Pacific Studies, Australian National University, Canberra.

Bowdler, S. (ed.) 1982. *Coastal archaeology in Eastern Australia.* Department of Prehistory, Australian National University, Canberra.

Bowdler, S. and S. O'Connor. 1991. The dating of the Australian Small Tool Tradition, with new evidence from the Kimberley, WA. *Australian Aboriginal Studies* 1991 No 1, pp 53–62.

Bowler, J.M., R. Jones, H. Allen and A.G. Thorne. 1970. Pleistocene human remains from Australia: a living site and cremation from Lake Mungo, western New South Wales. *World Archaeology* 2: 39–60.

Bowler, J.M., A.G. Thorne and H.A. Polach. 1972. Pleistocene man in Australia: age and significance of the Mungo skeleton. *Nature* 240: 48–50.

Bowler, J.M., A.G. Thorne and H.A. Polach. 1972. Prehistoric man at Lake Mungo by 32,000 years BP. *Nature* 240: 46–50.

Bowman, D.M. 1991. Can we untangle fire-megafauna-climate-human Pleistocene impacts on the Australian biota. *Archaeology in Oceania* 26: 78.

Breckwoldt, R. 1988. *A very elegant animal. The dingo.* Angus and Robertson, Sydney.

Brook, J. and J.L. Kohen. 1991. *The Parramatta Native Institution and the*

Black Town. A history. New South Wales University Press, Kensington.

Brown, P. 1981. Artificial cranial deformation: a component in the variation in Pleistocene Australian Aboriginal crania. *Archaeology in Oceania* 16(3): 156–67.

Brown, P. 1989. Coobal Creek. *Terra Australis* 13, Department of Prehistory, Research School of Pacific Studies, Australian National University, Canberra.

Bunney, S. 1990. First Australians 'were earliest seafarers'. *New Scientist* 19 May 1990, p 12.

Butlin, N. 1983. *Our original aggression*. George Allen and Unwin, Sydney.

Butlin, N. 1993. *Economics and the dreamtime. A hypothetical history*. Cambridge University Press, Cambridge.

Campbell, N.A. 1993. *Biology*. Benjamin/Cummings Publishing Company, Sydney.

Cann, R.L., M. Stoneking and A.C. Wilson. 1987. Mitochondrial DNA and human evolution. *Nature* 325: 31–6.

Catling, P.C. 1991. Ecological effects of prescribed burning practices on the mammals of southeastern Australia. In Lunney, D. (ed) *Conservation of Australia's forest fauna*. Royal Zoological Society of NSW, Mosman, pp 354–63.

Catling, P.C. and A.E. Newsome. 1981. Responses of the Australian vertebrate fauna to fire: an evolutionary approach. In A.M. Gill, R.H. Groves and I.R. Noble (eds) *Fire and the Australian biota*. Australian Academy of Science, Canberra.

Caughley, G., G.C. Grigg, J. Caughley and G.J.E. Hill. 1980. Does dingo predation control the densities of kangaroos and emus? *Australian Wildlife Research* 7: 1–2.

Chappell, J.M.A. and A. Grinrod (eds) CLIMANZ. 1981. *Proceedings of the first CLIMANZ conference, February 1981*. A symposium of results and discussions concerned with late Quaternary climatic history of Australia, New Zealand and surrounding areas. Department of Biogeography and Geomorphology, Research School of Pacific Studies, Australian National University, Canberra.

Christensen, P.E. and P.C. Kimber. 1975. Effects of prescribed burning on the flora and fauna of south-east Australian forests. *Proceedings of the Ecological Society of Australia* 9: 85–106.

Clark, G. 1978. *World prehistory in new perspective*. Cambridge University Press, Cambridge.

Clark, R.L. 1983. Pollen and charcoal evidence for the effects of Aboriginal burning on the vegetation of Australia. *Archaeology in Oceania* 18(1): 32–7.

Clark, S.S. and L. McLoughlin. 1986. Historical and biological evidence for fire regimes in the Sydney region prior to the arrival of Europeans. *Australian Geographer* 16: 101–12.

Clarke, A. 1994. Romancing the stones: the cultural construction of an archaeological landscape in the Western District of Victoria. *Archaeology in Oceania* 29(1): 1–15.

Cohen, M.N. 1977. *The food crisis in prehistory.* Yale University Press, New Haven.

Cosgrove, R. 1989. Thirty thousand years of human colonization in Tasmania: new Pleistocene dates. *Science* 243: 1706–8.

Coutts, P.J. F. 1978. The Keilor archaeological project. *Records of the Victorian Archaeological Survey* 8: 22–33.

Creagh, C. 1992. Looking after the land at Uluru. *Ecos* 71: 6–13.

Cribb, R., R. Walmberg, R. Wolmby and C. Taisman. 1988. Landscape as cultural artifact: shell mounds and plants in Aurukun, Cape York Peninsula. *Australian Aboriginal Studies* 1988 No 2, pp 60–73.

Cunningham, P. 1827. *Two years in New South Wales.* London.

Darwin, C. 1845 (1968). *The voyage of the Beagle.* Heron Books, Geneva.

Dayton, L. 1991. Melbourne skull may hold clues to origin of man. *New Scientist* 27 July 1991, p 8.

Dayton, L. 1992. Forest fires signal early arrival of first Australians. *New Scientist* 9 May 1992, p 7.

Dayton, L. 1994. The incredible shrinking Aborigines. *New Scientist* 2 April 1994, p 13.

Dickson, F.P. 1981. *Australian stone hatchets. A study in design and dynamics.* Academic Press, Sydney.

Dodson, J. (ed.) 1992. *The naive lands. Prehistory and environmental change in Australia and the Southwest Pacific.* Longman Cheshire, Melbourne.

Dodson, J., R. Fullagar, J. Furby, R. Jones and I. Prosser. 1993. Humans and megafauna in a late Pleistocene environment from Cuddie Springs, north western New South Wales. *Archaeology in Oceania* 28(2): 93–9.

Draper, N. 1987. Context for the Kartan: a preliminary report on excavations at Cape du Coeudic rockshelter, Kangaroo Island. *Archaeology in Oceania* 22(1): 1–8.

Duyker, E. 1983. Land use and ecological change in central New South Wales. *Journal of the Royal Australian Historical Society* 69(2): 120–32.

Etheridge, R., T.W. Edgeworth David and J. Grimshaw. 1896. On the occurrence of a submerged forest with remains of the dugong, at Shea's Creek, near Sydney. *Journal of the Royal Society of New South Wales* 30: 158–85.

Flannery, T. 1990. Pleistocene faunal loss: implications of the aftershock for Australia's past and future. *Archaeology in Oceania* 25: 45–67.

Flannery, T.F. and B. Gott. 1983. The Spring Creek locality, southwestern Victoria. A late surviving megafaunal assemblage. *Australian Zoologist* 21: 385–422

Flood, J. 1974. Pleistocene man at Clogg's Cave: his tool kit and environment. *Mankind* 9: 175–88.

Flood, J. 1980. *The moth hunters.* Australian Institute of Aboriginal Studies, Canberra.

Flood, J. 1983. *Archaeology of the Dreamtime.* Collins, Sydney.

Flood, J., B. David, J. Magee and B. English. 1987. Birrigai: a Pleistocene site in the southeastern highlands. *Archaeology in Oceania* 22: 9–26.

Fox, A. 1978. *The '72 fire of Nadgee Nature Reserve.* Parks and Wildlife 2: 5–24.

Fox, B.J. 1978. Temporal changes in a small mammal community on coastal heath regenerating after fire. *Bulletin of the Ecological Society of Australia* 8: 12–3.

Freedman, L. and M. Lofgren. 1979. The Cossack skull and dihybrid origin of the Australian Aborigines. *Nature* 282: 298–300.

Frith, H.J. and J.H. Calaby. 1969. *Kangaroos*. Cheshire, Melbourne.

Gamble, C. 1986. The artificial wilderness. *New Scientist*, 10 April 1986, pp 50–4.

Gee, H. 1992. Statistical cloud over African Eden. *Nature* 355: 583.

Gibbons, A. 1992. Mitochondrial Eve: wounded, but not yet dead. *Science* 257: 873–5.

Gill, A.M. 1974. Fire and the Australian Flora: a review. *Australian Forestry* 37: 4–25.

Gill, A.M., R.H. Groves and I.R. Noble (eds.) 1981. *Fire and the Australian biota*. Australian Academy of Science, Canberra.

Gillespie, R., D.R. Horton, P. Ladd, P.G. Macumber, T.H. Rich, R. Thorne and R.V.S. Wright. 1978. Lancefield Swamp and the extinction of the Australian megafauna. *Science* 200: 1044–8.

Goede, A. and P. Murray. 1977. Pleistocene man in south central Tasmania: evidence from a cave site in the Florentine Valley. *Mankind* 11: 2–10.

Gollan, K. 1984. The Australian dingo: in the shadow of man. In M. Archer and G. Clayton (eds.) *Vertebrate zoogeography — evolution in Australasia*. Hesperian Press, Carlisle, W.A.

Gorecki, P.P., D.R. Horton, N. Stern and R.V.S. Wright. 1984. Coexistence of humans and megafauna in Australia: improved stratigraphic evidence. *Archaeology in Oceania* 19(3): 117–9.

Gould, R.A. 1971. Uses and effects of fire among the western desert Aborigines of Australia. *Mankind* 8: 14–24.

Gray, A. 1985. Limits for demographic parameters of Aboriginal populations in the past. *Australian Aboriginal Studies* 1985 No 1, pp 22–7.

Guiler, E. 1985. *Thylacine. The tragedy of the Tasmanian Tiger*. Oxford University Press, Melbourne.

Hallam, S.J. 1975. *Fire and hearth. A study of Aboriginal usage and European usurpation in South-western Australia*. Australian Institute of Aboriginal Studies, Canberra.

Head, L. 1986. Palaeoecological contributions to Australian prehistory. *Archaeology in Oceania* 21(2): 121–9.

Head, L. 1989. Prehistoric Aboriginal impacts on Australian vegetation: an assessment of the evidence. *Australian Geographer* 20: 37–46.

Head, L. and R. Fullagar. 1991. 'We all la one land': pastoral excisions and Aboriginal resource use. *Australian Aboriginal Studies* 1991 No 1, pp 39–52.

Hickin, E.J. and K.J. Page. 1971. The age of valley fills in the Sydney Basin. *Search* 2(10): 383–4.

Hope, J.H., A. Dare-Edwards and M.L. McIntyre. 1983. Middens and megafauna: stratigraphy and dating of Lake Tandou lunette, Western New South Wales. *Archaeology in Oceania* 18: 45–52.

Horton, D.R. 1980. A review of the extinction question: man, climate and megafauna. *Archaeology and Physical Anthropology in Oceania* 15: 86–97.

Horton, D.R. 1981. Water and woodland: the peopling of Australia. *Newsletter of the Australian Institute of Aboriginal Studies* 16: 21–7.

Horton, D.R. 1982. The burning question: Aborigines, fire and Australian ecosystems. *Mankind* 13(3): 237–51.

Hughes, P.J. 1980. Thesis abstract. The geomorphology of archaeological sites on the south coast of New South Wales. *Australian Archaeology* 11: 50–2.

Hughes, P.J. and R.J. Lampert. 1982. Prehistoric population change in southern coastal New South Wales. In S. Bowdler (ed) 1982. *Coastal archaeology in Eastern Australia.* Department of Prehistory, Australian National University, Canberra.

Hughes, P.J and M.E. Sullivan. 1981. Aboriginal burning and late Holocene geomorphic events. *Search* 12: 277–8.

Hynes, R.A. and A.K. Chase. 1982. Plants, sites and domiculture: Aboriginal influence upon plant communities in Cape York Peninsula. *Archaeology in Oceania* 17: 38–50.

Isaacs, J. 1987. *Bush food: Aboriginal food and herbal medicine.* Ure Smith Press, Sydney.

Jones, R. 1969. Firestick farming. *Australian Natural History* 16: 224–8.

Jones, R. 1971. Rocky Cape and the problem of the Tasmanians. Unpublished PhD thesis, University of Sydney.

Jones, R. 1974. Tasmanian tribes. In N.B. Tindale *Aboriginal tribes of Australia.* University of California Press, Berkeley.

Kamminga, J. 1978. Journey into the microcosms. Unpublished PhD thesis, University of Sydney.

Kefous, K. 1977. We have a fish with ears and wonder if it is valuable? Unpublished BA (Hons) thesis, Department of Prehistory and Anthropology, Australian National University, Canberra.

Kershaw, A.P. 1986. Climatic change and Aboriginal burning in north-east Australia during the last two glacial/interglacial cycles. *Nature* 322: 47–9.

Kershaw, A.P. 1993. Palynology, biostratigraphy and human impact. *The Artefact* 16: 12–18.

Kiernan, K., R. Jones and D. Ranson. 1983. New evidence from Fraser Cave for glacial age man in south-west Tasmania. *Nature* 301: 28–32.

Kimber, R.G. 1976. Beginnings of farming? Some man-plant-animal relationships in Central Australia. *Mankind* 10: 145–50.

Kimber, R.G. 1984. Resource use and management in central Australia. *Australian Aboriginal Studies*, 1984 No 2, pp 12–23.

Knudtson, P. and D. Suzuki. 1992. *Wisdom of the elders.* Allen and Unwin, Sydney.

Kodela, P.G. and J.R. Dodson. 1988. A late Holocene vegetation and fire record from Ku-ring-Gai Chase National Park. *Proceedings of the Linnean Society of New South Wales* 110(4): 315–26.

Kohen, J.L. 1985. *Aborigines in the west. Prehistory to present.* Western Sydney Project Monograph, Nepean College of Advanced Education, Kingswood.

Kohen, J.L. 1986. *Prehistoric settlement in the western Cumberland Plain: resources, environment and technology.* Unpublished PhD thesis, Macquarie University, Sydney.

Kohen, J.L. 1988. The Dharug of the western Cumberland Plain: ethnography and demography. In B. Meehan and R. Jones (eds) *Archaeology with ethnography. An Australian perspective.* Department of Prehistory, Research School of Pacific Studies, Australian National University, Canberra.

Kohen, J.L. 1993. *The Darug and their neighbours. The traditional Aboriginal owners of the Sydney region.* Darug Link in association with Blacktown and District Historical Society, Blacktown.

Kohen, J.L. and A.J. Downing. 1992. Aboriginal use of plants on the western Cumberland Plain. *Sydney Basin Naturalist* 1: 1–8.

Kohen, J.L. and R.J. Lampert. 1987. Hunters and fishers of the Sydney region. In D.J. Mulvaney and J.P. White (eds) *Australians to 1788.* Fairfax, Syme and Weldon, Sydney.

Kohen, J.L., E.D. Stockton and M.A.J. Williams. 1984. Shaws Creek KII rockshelter: a prehistoric occupation site in the Blue Mountains piedmont, eastern New South Wales. *Archaeology in Oceania* 19(2): 57–73.

Lampert, R.J. 1971a. Burrill Lake and Currarong. *Terra Australis* 1, Department of Prehistory, Research School of Pacific Studies, Australian National University, Canberra.

Lampert, R.J. 1971b. Coastal Aborigines of southeastern Australia. In D.J. Mulvaney and J. Golson (eds) *Aboriginal man and environment in Australia.* Australian National University Press, Canberra.

Lampert, R.J. 1981. The great Kartan mystery. *Terra Australis* 5. Research School of Pacific Studies, Australian National University, Canberra.

Lampert, R.J. 1983a. The Kartan mystery revisited. *Australian Archaeology* 16: 175–7.

Lampert, R.J. 1983b. Waisted Blades in Australia? *Records of the Australian Museum* 35: 145–51.

Lampert, R.J. and P.J. Hughes. 1980. Pleistocene archaeology in the Flinders Ranges. Research prospects. *Australian Archaeology* 10: 11–20.

Lampert, R.J. and F. Sanders. 1973. Plants and men on the Beecroft Peninsula, New South Wales. *Mankind* 9: 96–108.

Lawrence, R. 1991. Motorised transport in remote Aboriginal Australia. *Australian Aboriginal Studies* 1991 No 2, pp 62–6.

Leubbers, R. 1975. Ancient boomerangs discovered in South Australia. *Nature* 253:39.

Lewin, R. 1987. The masking of Mitochondrial Eve. *Science* 238: 24–6.

Lewin, R. 1990. Molecular clock runs out of time. *New Scientist* 10 February 1990.

Lewin, R. 1991. DNA evidence strengthens Eve hypothesis. *New Scientist* 19 October 1991, p 16.

Lister, A.M. 1989. Rapid dwarfing of red deer on Jersey in the Last Interglacial. *Nature* 342: 539–42.

Lourandos, H. 1977. Aboriginal spatial organization and population: south western Victoria reconsidered. *Archaeology and Physical Anthropology in Oceania* 12: 202–25.

Lourandos, H. 1980. Change or stability? Hydraulics, hunter-gatherers and population in temperate Australia. *World Archaeology* 11: 245–66.

Lourandos, H. 1983. 10,000 years in the Tasmanian Highlands. *Australian Archaeology* 16: 39–47.

Macintosh, N.W.G. 1971. Analysis of an Aboriginal skeleton and a pierced tooth necklace from Lake Nitchie, Australia. *Anthropologie* 9: 49–62.

Macknight, C.C. 1976. *The voyage to Marege.* Melbourne University Press, Melbourne.

Macumber, P.G. and R. Thorne. 1975. The Cohuna cranium site — a reappraisal. *Archaeology and Physical Anthropology in Oceania* 10: 65–70.

Martin, H.A. 1978. Evolution of the Australian flora and vegetation through the Tertiary: evidence from pollen. *Alcheringa* 2: 181–202.

Martin, P.S. and R.G. Klein (eds) 1984. *Quaternary extinctions. A prehistoric revolution.* University of Arizona Press, Tucson.

Martin, R. 1994. Of Koalas, Tree-Kangaroos and Men. *Australian Natural History* 24(3): 23–31.

Marun, L.H. 1972. The Mirning and their predecessors on the coastal Nullarbor Plain. Unpublished PhD thesis, Department of Anthropology, University of Sydney.

McCarthy, F.D. 1964. The archaeology of the Capertee Valley, New South Wales. *Records of the Australian Museum* 26(6): 197–246.

Meehan, B. 1982. *Shell bed to shell midden.* Australian Institute of Aboriginal Studies, Canberra.

Meehan, B. and R. Jones (eds) 1988. *Archaeology with ethnography. An Australian perspective.* Department of Prehistory, Research School of Pacific Studies, Australian National University, Canberra.

Meggitt, M.J. 1962. *Desert people. A study of the Walbiri Aborigines of Central Australia.* Angus and Robertson, Sydney.

Mitchell, T.L. 1848. *Journal of an expedition into the interior of tropical Australia.* Longman, Brown, Green and Longmans, London.

Mulvaney, D.J. 1975. *The prehistory of Australia.* Penguin Press, Blackburn.

Mulvaney, D.J. and J. Golson (eds) 1971. *Aboriginal man and environment in Australia.* Australian National University Press, Canberra.

Mulvaney, D.J. and J.P. White (eds) 1987. *Australians to 1788.* Fairfax, Syme and Weldon, Sydney.

Nanson, G.C., R. Young and E. Stockton. 1987. Chronology and palaeoenvironment of the Cranebrook Terrace (near Sydney) containing artefacts more than 40,000 years old. *Archaeology in Oceania.* 22: 72–8.

Newsome, A.E. and P.C. Catling. 1983. The feeding ecology of the dingo II. Dietary and numerical relationships with fluctuating prey populations in Southeastern Australia. *Australian Journal of Ecology* 8: 345–66.

Newsome, A.E., L.K. Corbett, P.C. Catling and R.J. Burt. 1983. The stomach contents of trapped dingoes and the catching of non-target wildlife in dingo traps in Southeastern Australia. *Australian Wildlife Research* 10: 477–86.

Noble, I.R. and R.O. Slatyer. 1981. Concepts and models of succession in vascular plant communities subject to recurrent fire. In A.M. Gill, R.H. Groves and I.R. Noble (eds) *Fire and the Australian biota*. Australian Academy of Science, Canberra.

O'Connor, S. 1989. Contemporary island use in the west Kimberley, Western Australia, and its implications for archaeological site survival. *Australian Aboriginal Studies* 1989 No 2, pp 25–31.

O'Dea, K., J. Naughton, A. Sinclair, L. Rabuco and R. Smith. 1987. Lifestyle change and nutritional status in Kimberley Aborigines. *Australian Aboriginal Studies* 1987 No 1, pp 46–51.

Pain, S. 1988. The healthiest restaurant in Australia. *New Scientist* 18 August 1988, pp 42–7.

Palmer, L.J. 1993. Blood residue detection: an Australian appraisal. In B.L. Fankhauser and J.R. Bird (eds) *Archaeometry. Current Australasian research*. Occasional Papers in Prehistory No 22. Department of Prehistory, Research School of Pacific Studies, Australian National University, Canberra.

Pearce, R.H. and M. Barbetti. 1981. A 38,000-year-old archaeological site at Upper Swan, Western Australia. *Archaeology in Oceania* 16(3): 173–6.

Peterson, N. 1986. *Australian territorial organisation*. Oceania Monograph 30, University of Sydney.

Phillip, A. 1789. *The voyage of Governor Phillip to Botany Bay*. London.

Pocock, C. 1988. An analysis of the faunal remains from the Miriwun rock-shelter, Ord Basin, east Kimberley. B.A. (Hons) thesis, Department of Archaeology, University of Western Australia, Perth.

Pyne, S.J. 1991. *Burning bush. A fire history of Australia*. Henry Holt and Co., New York.

Radcliffe-Brown, A.R. 1930. Former numbers and distribution of the Australian Aborigines. *Official yearbook of the Commonwealth of Australia*. Australian Government Publishing Service, Canberra.

Roberts, R.G., R. Jones and M.A. Smith. 1990. Themoluminescence dating of a 50,000-year-old human occupation site in northern Australia. *Nature* 345: 153–6.

Ross, A. 1981. Holocene environments and prehistoric site patterning in the Victorian Mallee. *Archaeology in Oceania* 16: 145–54.

Rowland, M.J. 1983. Aborigines and environments in holocene Australia: changing paradigms. *Australian Aboriginal Studies* 1983 No 2, pp 62–77.

Russell-Smith, J. 1985. A record of change: studies of Holocene vegetation history in the South Alligator Region, Northern Territory. *Proceedings of the Ecological Society of Australia* 13: 191–202.

Saul, H. 1992. How humans massacred the mammoths. *New Scientist* 2 May 1992, p 14.

Schrire, C. 1982. The Alligator Rivers: prehistory and ecology in western

Arnhem Land. *Terra Australis* 7. Department of Prehistory, Research School of Pacific Studies, Australian National University, Canberra.

Singh, G., A.P. Kershaw and R. Clark. 1981. Quaternary vegetation and fire history in Australia. In A.M. Gill, R.H. Groves and I.R. Noble (eds) *Fire and the Australian biota*. Australian Academy of Science, Canberra.

Singh, G. and E.A. Geissler. 1985. Late Cainozoic history of vegetation, fire, lake levels and climate, at Lake George, New South Wales, Australia. *Philosophical Transactions of the Royal Society London*, 311: 379–447.

Singh, G., N.D. Opdyke and J.M. Bowler. 1981. Late Cainozoic stratigraphy, palaeomagnetic chronology and vegetation history from Lake George, NSW. *Journal of the Geological Society of Australia* 28: 435–52.

Smith, M.A. 1986. The antiquity of seedgrinding in arid central Australia. *Archaeology in Oceania* 21: 29–39.

Smith, M.A. 1989. The case for a resident human population in the Central Australian Ranges during full glacial aridity. *Archaeology in Oceania* 24(3): 93–105.

Smith, M.A., M. Spriggs and B. Fankhauser (eds). 1993. *Sahul in review*. Department of Prehistory, Research School of Pacific Studies, Australian National University, Canberra.

Specht, R.L. 1981. Responses to fires in heathlands and related shrublands. In A.M. Gill, R.H. Groves and I.R. Noble (eds) *Fire and the Australian Biota*. Australian Academy of Science, Canberra.

Stockton, E.D. 1970. An archaeological survey of the Blue Mountains. *Mankind* 7(4): 295–301.

Stockton, E.D. and W.N. Holland. 1974. Cultural sites and their environment in the Blue Mountains. *Archaeology and Physical Anthropology in Oceania* 9: 36–65.

Stringer, C. 1990. The emergence of modern humans. *Scientific American* December 1990, pp 68–74.

Stringer, C.B. and P. Andrews. 1988. Genetic and fossil evidence for the origin of modern humans. *Science* 239: 1263–8.

Sullivan, M.E. 1976. Archaeological occupation site locations on the south coast of New South Wales. *Archaeology and Physical Anthropology in Oceania* 11: 56–69.

Thomas, I. 1993. Late Pleistocene environments and Aboriginal settlement patterns in Tasmania. *Australian Archaeology* 36: 1–11.

Thorne, A.G. and P.G. Macumber. 1972. Discoveries of late Pleistocene man at Kow Swamp, Australia. *Nature* 238: 316–19.

Thorne, A.G. and R. Raymond. 1989. *Man on the rim. The peopling of the Pacific*. Angus and Robertson, Sydney.

Thorne, A.G. and M.H. Wolpoff. 1992. The multiregional evolution of humans. *Scientific American* April 1992, pp 28–33.

Tindale, N.B. 1937. Relationship of the extinct Kangaroo Island Culture with cultures of Australia, Tasmania, and Malaya. *Records of the South Australian Museum* 6: 39–60.

Tindale, N.B. 1974. *Aboriginal tribes of Australia*. University of California Press, Berkeley.

Tindale-Biscoe, H. 1975. *Life of marsupials.* Edward Arnold Australia, Port Melbourne.

Vanderwal, R. 1978. Adaptive technology in southwest Tasmania. *Australian Archaeology* 8: 107–26.

Vartanyan, S.L., V.E. Garutt and A.V. Sher. 1993. Holocene dwarf mammoths from Wrangel Island in the Siberian Arctic. *Nature* 362: 337–40.

Veth, P. 1989. Islands in the interior: a model for the colonization of Australia's arid zone. *Archaeology in Oceania* 24(3): 81–92.

Veth, P.M. and F.J. Walsh. 1988. The concept of 'staple' plant foods in the Western Desert region of Western Australia. *Australian Aboriginal Studies* 1988 No 2, pp 19–25.

Vickers-Rich, P., J.M. Monaghan, R.F. Baird and T.H. Rich (eds) 1991. *Vertebrate palaeontology of Australasia.* Pioneer Design Studios in cooperation with the Monash University Publications Committee, Melbourne.

Walker, J. 1981. Fuel dynamics in Australian vegetation. In A.M. Gill, R.H. Groves and I.R. Noble (eds) *Fire and the Australian biota.* Australian Academy of Science, Canberra.

Webb, S.G. 1989. *The Willandra Lakes Hominids.* Department of Prehistory, Research School of Pacific Studies, Australian National University, Canberra.

White, J.P. and J.F. O'Connell. 1979. Australian prehistory: new aspects of antiquity. *Science* 203: 21–8.

White, J.P. and J.F. O'Connell. 1982. *A prehistory of Australia, New Guinea and Sahul.* Academic Press, Sydney.

White, M.A. 1986. *The greening of Gondwana.* Reed Books.

Wilson, A.C. and R.L. Cann. 1992. The recent African genesis of humans. *Scientific American* April 1992, pp 22–7.

Winter, J.W. 1970. How many roos can a roo-shooter shoot and still have roos to shoot? *Wildlife in Australia* 7: 34–7.

Wolpoff, M. and A. Thorne. 1991. The case against Eve. *New Scientist* 22 June 1991, pp 33–7.

Wright, R. 1986a. New light on the extinction of the Australian megafauna. *Proceedings of the Linnaean Society of New South Wales* 109: 1–9.

Wright, R. 1986b. How old is zone F at Lake George? *Archaeology in Oceania* 21(2): 138–9.

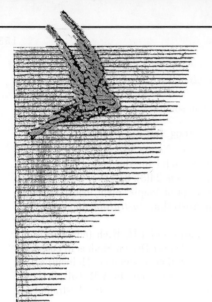

Index